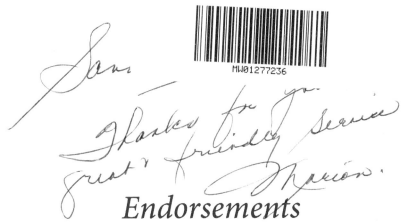

Endorsements

80 Years By Faith

My wife and I have known the Petersons for many years. We were privileged to sit under their ministry as young Bible College students when they came home from the foreign field on furlough and ministered in Bible Temple (now Mannahouse). Who'd have guessed that in God's providence we would be afforded the blessing of working side by side with them as elders in a church my wife and I planted after college.

Lew and Marion's heart for the world, and for being people of vision, was as strong in their later years as when we first observed them on the mission field. Their deposit in our lives is immeasurable. They were and are truly an inspiration for anyone who wants to live God-sized dreams.

—Derrill and Michal Corbin
Executive Pastors, Mannahouse Global

~ ~ ~

I have had the privilege of knowing Lew and Marion Peterson my entire life. Even more so, I am grateful for the imprint of their lives on my heart. They were my youth pastors, my heart encouragers, and my fellow worship warriors. Without a doubt, Lew and Marion Peterson always pursued God with an undiluted passion.

Very few people have been blessed with such a rich heritage regarding the presence of God—Lew and Marion are counted amongst those few. As such, Marion is well qualified to articulate what it is and what it takes to have the heart of a Presence Pursuer. Her journey is a treasured roadmap for all who would hunger for such a heritage. I count it a privilege to be one of her "sons in the faith," to have digested the priceless account of her life story, and to be considered a part of her legacy as a passionate pursuer of His Presence.

—Howard Rachinski, Author
Founder, Christian Copyright Licensing International (CCLI)

~   ~   ~

Adventure! Joy! History! Friendship! Trauma! Jesus! Stories...

All of this and much, much more is written in this delightful book written by my dear friend, Marion Peterson. Our families share history for over seven decades, and through the travels of life we have kept in touch.

Many of these stories are new to me, and they thrummed my heart strings with an emotional response that surprised me. In each of these adventures and lessons learned, we see the joyous hand of God. Read this book, and see both the strength of purpose and the hand of God.

—Ethel Goward Burns
College Instructor, Teacher

~   ~   ~

It has been my privilege to know Marion Peterson, along with her late husband Lew, for over 35 years. Their dynamic mission work in Uganda was inspiring to many around the world. The primary focus of their return to North America was continued, faithful ministry to church leaders and congregations. Marion has captured a piece of the inspiration and dynamism of those years in this book.

—Terry S. Clark, Executive VP
VTO Labs, Colorado

This book will inspire and bless you abundantly. I have known Marion Peterson for over 60 years—even as a teenage girl named Marion Layzell, before she married Lew Peterson. As daughter to an Apostle of the Restoration movement that was spreading throughout the world in the 1950's, Marion was raised to be a dedicated Christian, a student of the Word of God, and a zealous worshipper of the Lord Jesus.

Marion and Lew pastored for many years and served as missionaries in Uganda, Africa for over a decade. As your read her story and discover the truths she shares, be open to a greater love for the Lord and a zeal to serve and worship Jesus more passionately.

Marion is one of the most dedicated Christian ministers you could ever meet. It's good that you have this book in your hand now. It has the potential to make you an even greater son or daughter of God. Bless you, Marion, for sharing your life with the Body of Christ.

—Bishop Bill Hamon, Author
Bishop, Christian International Apostolic-Global Network

~ ~ ~

I thank God for special people who are fearless, who see an impossibility as an opportunity, and who dare to believe their God. Thank God for those teachers and preachers of the Word who are not afraid to put their shoulder to the task, caring not whose name is on the credit rolls. Such are Lew and Marion Peterson—selfless, sacrificing, anointed, and grounded teachers of the Word with a prophetic edge.

For over 40 years they have impacted our lives like few others. Thank you for carrying the call and vision, for laboring tirelessly, and for loving and pouring into people over and over again, always with eternity in view. You have dared to stand against the bear, the lion, and yes, the taunting Goliaths. Your foundations of worship, your zeal for the Tabernacle of David and your passion for the house of the Lord have impacted not only my life and our church, but nations around the world.

This is the testimony of two young hearts who, with bright futures ahead of them, heard the call of God and were willing to give up the best years of their lives "for the best years of their lives." Reading the life story of two of God's finest, you will also be drawn into the very spirit of their journey.

From youth pastors to church planters, from missionaries to Bible College founders, Lew and Marion answered the call. Their deep love for Jesus and burning hearts for souls through years of service, testing, joys, disappointments and victories, are evidenced on every page.

Rev. 1:19 says, "write it down . . . write it down." Well, here it is.

Laurence and Iris Hueppelsheuser
Pastors, People's Church

~ ~ ~

Marion and I met when we were 6 years old. We made a commitment together to follow Jesus, and Marion's faith has never faltered. She has been faithful to His call on her life. You will love this book of adventure in God's mercy and grace.

—Margaret Inglis Lynn
Business Administration

~ ~ ~

When I was growing up, our home was a gathering place, filled with people sharing their stories. In writing this book Mom has invited you into the home of her heart. My parents' joy in serving God wherever they lived, and in whatever role they were assigned, impacted my life deeply. Mom's memories are all here: the victories, the lessons and the challenges throughout her life. Let it inspire you the way it continues to inspire me.

— Mari Lou Holmes
Daughter

80 Years By Faith

MARION LAYZELL-PETERSON

80
Years
By Faith

MARION LAYZELL-PETERSON
© 2020

All Rights Reserved
ISBN: 9798632012294

Dedication

I must introduce you to my Dad, Reg Layzell. We will find him often throughout these chapters, as he played a major part in our lives. He was my Father, and Mari Lou's Grandfather, as well as our Pastor/Apostle. Dad was a man to be respected and a leader of leaders. To him I dedicate *80 Years By Faith.*

Reg was seldom wrong, and most of the time if he was wrong, he would not admit it! His actions would demonstrate he knew he was wrong, and a twinkle would appear in his eyes. The corners of his mouth would shimmer as he tried not to smile, but we knew it said to us, "I'm sorry." In my thinking he was always right. Actually, I believe he thought his actions, instructions and criticisms were character building, and they probably were.

Often we clashed. Folk told me all the time, "You are just like your Dad." They meant it as a compliment, but I hated hearing it. I didn't want to be like him! Later in life I realized that they were talking about his character, whereas I was thinking personality.

Dad, whose father was a graduate of Surgeon's College in London, England, was raised a Baptist. He was disillusioned with the lack of biblical fulfillment in the church and declared himself an Atheist. In 1932 (the "hungry thirties") Dad met Jesus in a very real way, and his world totally changed. He was changed from an angry, bitter young man to a true disciple of Jesus with a passion to build the Church of Jesus Christ, which he did for 52 years with great focus.

Through the years his personality didn't change much, although he did become "softer" in his senior years. He smiled more, relaxed, and enjoyed his family more. After Mother passed away, he was lost—probably with some regrets, because she had a few travelling desires that he had been too preoccupied to fulfill for her. At her memorial service he stood by her coffin, looked down at her and said, "Nellie, you loved, and you won!" The "if only" regrets were very real in his heart as he shared them with Lew, which made us realize how loving his heart really was. After we had cleared up all Mother's matters, he was leaving to be with my brother in eastern Canada, and we were leaving for Uganda. He hugged and kissed me goodbye, and for the first time in my life, I heard him say, "I love you, Marion!" I was 46 years old!

One of Dad's strong characteristics was his self discipline, and he endeavored to pass that on to his children, grandchildren and great grandchildren, and as well as to every church he was involved with. My conclusion is that he succeeded in a measure, without them or him realizing it, and that in the end it benefited us all. At times we were "mad as hops" at him—maybe hurt and offended—but unconsciously he was passing on something in his character that he deemed important. From the positive outcome of his children and the following generations, I think we learned our lessons well. Of course, we have modified it some as the generations have come along, but the principles taught have remained in each of our DNA.

In short, whatever we accomplished through our lives was because of Reg Layzell. We will always be thankful for all he was and everything he did to be certain that, as children, we became true disciples of Jesus Christ. Then he continually guided us in understanding our destiny in the Kingdom of God.

Thank you, Dad!

Table of Contents

Preface

Welcome to the lifetime of adventures of Lewis and Marion Peterson. The vision and passion God gave us became everything that motivated and guided us through our life together. God made us strong disciples, determined to fulfill everything in His plan for us. We didn't do a perfect job, but we tried to the best of our understanding.

"Going steady" in our teen years, we became best friends, involved together in almost every church activity while we finished school. Lew became a brick mason, and I was a cosmetologist. Later we both received our BA in Theology through Christian International, Santa Rosa Beach, Florida.

During our 59 years of marriage we changed addresses on an average of every 2½ years! The longest we were in one place—which included five street addresses—was Uganda, where we spent a total of 17 years (half of all the years of our ministry).

Years ago, at a prayer conference in City Bible Church, Portland, Oregon, one of the visiting speakers said to me, "Marion, write your story." That wasn't the first time I'd heard that admonition. Then again through the years, I heard it so many times. We found ourselves telling stories of our adventures while ministering in various countries, at churches or visiting with friends: "You need to record this, Marion. Write a book." Who, me? *Write a book? I am not a writer. I am lucky to be able to spell my own name!*

Lew had developed his thesis on "The Cross" into a college course and seminar teachings, so we finally put it all together and published *It's Still the Cross* in 2010. It is available through Amazon and on Kindle.

As our grandsons grew up hearing our stories, they would beg us over and over again, "Gramps, tell us the story about such and such again." When we were together with them, their friends would ask, "Tell so and so about the time that such and such happened." Lew and I talked about writing so many times. We made plans, wrote notes, and even thought about potential titles and chapter ideas, but that is as far as it went.

My desire to document our life has been deep down in my heart for decades, but I didn't seem to have the needed inspiration to get started. I really doubted my ability, and neither Lew nor I had never been a journaling person. I have only our messages and teaching notes, and my memories with the consultation of family and longtime friends. I didn't want to write just an autobiography of stories and happenings, but a book that would express our life and our heart passion.

I don't presume to be a professional writer, but the inspiration to get started finally came. My only hesitation was that Lew is not here. With this mulling around in my brain, one early morning I awoke— and the inspiration was there! Automatic question: *How will I do this without him?* Then, whirling around in my head were Lew's famous words of encouragement, spoken to me so many times through the years: "Great idea. Yes, you can do it."

Acknowledgements

To my wonderful long-time friends, Jim and Laura Davis. They taught me, encouraged me, loved me even in my mistakes, and advised me. They simply kept going with this inexperienced writer that was discovering how, in a new way and a new season, to express herself.

Thank you both so much. It was difficult at times when living in different countries, but thanks to your knowledge in the cyber world and even with busy schedules you were always there for me, honest and loving. I don't have sufficient words to express how much I appreciate you both.

Abundant Blessings and Thank you.

Introduction

How does it go?

- "You get too late smart and too soon old."
- "Senior years are not golden, they are just plain brass."
- "It takes a brave person to get old."

But then, there are a lot folk who don't have the opportunity to grow old! I think "old" is not where we are chronologically—*but* I try to think this way:

- I look after myself. "How am I doing physically, mentally and health-wise?"
- Stay positive, not negative. Focus on what is good. "What are my meditations?"
- Am I listening to what God is saying, serving and accepting this generation? "Do I keep moving on?"

In addition, I remind myself:

- "Hey, I'm still alive. I have all the tools to accomplish His purpose in me at this season of my life."
- "Rejoice and be glad!"

Lately I've been meditating on God's goodness through the years. Lew and I had 65 years of wonderful adventures together—first as teens, then 59 years married, pastoring, and traveling in many countries. We met many wonderful people and enjoyed many years of team ministry together, fulfilling our dream in Uganda, East Africa as missionary pastors. We had fun in the valleys and on the mountain tops, and also in between while climbing!

His Name has been my strong tower and I have run into it and been safe. My heart sings the powerful old hymn . . .

All hail the Power of Jesus Name,
Let angels prostrate fall,
Bring forth the royal diadem
And crown Him Lord of all.

I am a child of God, in His family, His disciple, and I am called by His name: "Christian." There is *redeeming power* in the Name of Jesus, and that includes all the benefits of His powerful Name.

Let every kindred, every tribe
On this terrestrial ball,
To him all majesty ascribe,
And crown Him Lord of all.
—Edward Perronet, 1780

I pray with Jesus, "…that they all may be one that the world may believe… " in the power of the redemptive grace in His Name.

His Grace has always been sufficient, amazing, and so comforting when we had our challenges throughout our journey.

Wonderful Grace of Jesus,
Greater than all my sin,
How shall my tongue describe it,
Where shall his praise begin?

Taking away my burden,
Setting my spirit free;
For the wonderful grace of Jesus
Reaches me.
— Haldor Lillenas, 1918

On one of our trips into the Congo, we headed for the church that was on the top of the mountains. We parked our car, walked to the base of the mountain to cross the river, and begin climbing, but found the "bridge" to be a barely 12-foot-wide, very round log!

"Grace, Lord. Please, Mighty God, how can I do this. Surely you don't expect me to walk across that?"

Lew encouraged me. A brave man, a fully pastoral, godly counselor! "You can do it!"

"Sure! Okay for you to say!"

We crossed it, and began to climb for two hours to Sunday morning church at the top! George, our interpreter, had my accordion on his head. Lew was fighting malaria, so we prayed, "Jehovah Rapha, we need your healing here." I am not, and never have been a hiker or climber. I put one foot in front of the other, thinking my lungs would pop out of my body. Not really, but I was certainly breathing hard!

Help me, Jesus. You are my King, the Lord of my life. You are in control. Please show me your strength to finish this climb.

Up, up we went for two hours on the rocky path, finally hearing the singing of the waiting believers above us. People were sitting on rocks and logs, and they were so happy to see us. I was a spectacle—a blonde, blue eyed woman. They had never seen one! They touched my hair, stared into my eyes, pinched my skin, and laughed and chatted all about me, and I couldn't understand a word they said!

Let me rest, Lord. Please let your peace wash over me. Let my heart beat normally again. I need a good dose of your Peace and Grace.

Wonderful grace of Jesus,
Reaching to all the lost.
By it I have been pardoned,
Saved to the uttermost.
Chains have been torn asunder,
Giving me liberty,
For the wonderful grace of Jesus
Reaches me!

To finish my story, we were invited for tea in a very small, stuffy hut. Sitting there, I realized I needed to find an outhouse, and Lew was not doing well. He needed air so we excused ourselves together and went looking. We found a reed shack that they had lovingly made for the white visitors. It was perched on the rocks, where a crack in the rock became the hole! The door was a small piece of sack, and certainly not as wide as the door!

"Wonderful?!"

"Go ahead—I will keep watch," Lew said.

There is a first time for everything. So I prepared myself, breathing slowly, trying to hurry, but not realizing that slowly by slowly the whole shack was beginning to roll to the edge of the mountain, and picking up speed! I screamed, "Lewis!"

He grabbed my arm, I grabbed my clothes, and he dragged me out as the shack continued down to its freedom! I was so glad it was Lew outside that shack, not the interpreter who usually watched over me like a hawk when we were in a different place.

All was well. We survived, cleaned up, and went back to finish our tea. We continued our visit with a great service. I was thrilled as the sound of voices worshipping Jesus echoed across the tops of the Congo mountains and His Word was preached to everyone within hearing distance.

I thanked Jesus for watching over me as I relaxed in His presence. God was with us all the time, no matter where we were or what we were doing. He is our Shepherd. He leads us. We are and do what we do because he leads us in good pastures. He is my Everlasting Father and cares about me always.

Wonderful Grace of Jesus,
Reaching the most defiled.
By its transforming power,
Making him God's dear child.
Purchasing peace and heaven
For all eternity,
And the wonderful grace of Jesus
Reaches me.

With the thought of the power of redemptive grace, my desire in writing this book is to write about His awesome Grace that redeemed me and gave me all I need in order to know Him as my Father, Savior, Friend, and the Lord of my Life. I have enjoyed many benefits of the power in His Name, with His Grace undergirding me as I walked my life journey of adventures.

You are welcome to enjoy my adventures with me. Please be thankful with me for His Grace, and for the indwelling power in His Name that helped me to enjoy the journey!

Wonderful the matchless grace of Jesus,
Deeper than the mighty rolling sea,
Higher than the mountain,
Sparkling like a fountain,
All sufficient grace for even me.
Broader that the scope of my transgression,
Greater far than all my sin and shame,
Oh, magnify the precious name of Jesus,
Praise His Name!
—Haldor Lillenas 1918

Enjoy!
Marion

CHAPTER ONE

Mukama Wange
(My Lord)

Y ou see, because of my family I had known about Jesus since I was four, and I had known Him as my Savior since I was six years old. I grew up knowing about Him—all about Him—going to church, reading the Bible, saying my prayers, and grace at the table. I could have gone on like that, but my Father was very wise. One day he said to me, "Marion, you cannot know Jesus just because your Mother and I do. You must know Him as your own Savior by asking Him into your heart yourself. Then you will be saved and will go to Heaven." So I did—the next Sunday when the altar call was given.

But that was not enough. In a rough, early-teen moment I decided I was done with all the discipline stuff and ready to run away. So I went to our youth leader Thelma and tearfully told her my grievances.

She said, "Go home, kneel bedside your bed, and cry out to Jesus to help you do what is His will."

I did just that, with buckets of frustrated, angry tears, and when the storm was over I opened my Bible. It fell open to Psalm 16 and my eyes fell on verse 11 (KJV).

"Thou wilt show me the path of life,
in thy presence is fullness of joy
and at thy right hand
there are pleasures forevermore."

I had my answer! This became my life scripture. I went to it every time the old rebellion would rise, and I began to develop a deep love for Jesus, My Lord. His presence became my focus. I found not only happiness, but joy in His presence—full and indescribable joy. Then the pleasure that I craved came as I submitted myself to living a disciplined life in His plan and purpose.

I developed a positive, happy attitude toward my life. I began to understand that what I had was His joy, not my own! In this life, if I depended on being happy I would be disappointed. But if I leaned into His joy and His presence, I would experience the true joy.

At this time I also discovered that love and His joy were connected, and in my indecision love won, and the joy came. I had accepted Him as my Savior when I prayed with my Pastor at six years old, but now I discovered he wanted to be my Lord. I believed and did all the right things as I was taught, because it was right, but that day as a 14 year-old teen, I fell in love with Jesus, and everything changed. Suddenly life wasn't so bad. Being at church all the time stopped being a chore. (I knew everything about church, so why am I here all the time?) But now, being there was a pleasure.

I found myself singing, and song became my greatest joy. It was the era of Elvis Presley and the Beatles, but I knew nothing about them or their music except what I heard at school. I fell in love with singing about Jesus, and that produced His presence in my soul and spirit. He is my song. I laugh, I cry, I dance, I worship, I clap, I jump, I just love being in His presence singing the Song!

You may have the joy-bells ringing in your heart,
And a peace that from you never will depart;
Walk the straight and narrow way,
Live for Jesus every day,
He will keep the joy-bells ringing in your heart.
—J. Edwin Ruark (1893)

From time to time I find myself singing songs we sang in Sunday School so many years ago.

JOY, joy, I have found joy.
I'll sing it and shout it, tell others about it,
Till no one can doubt it that I have found JOY!

In Nehemiah's adventure of rebuilding the ancient walls of Jerusalem, when the folk remembered what it was like at home in years past and began weeping, Nehemiah declared to them,

"This day is holy to the Lord, do not mourn nor weep.
Go your way, eat the fat, drink the sweet,
send portions to those for whom nothing is prepared:
for this day is holy to our Lord. Do not sorrow,
for the JOY of the Lord is your strength."
—Nehemiah 8:9–10

In this day the conclusion is that enough "stuff," secure finances, and circumstances bring us the joy we long for. In some way the recession brought big challenges to most of us. Lay-offs came as surprises, no jobs were to be found, savings were depleted, some of us lost our homes, and along with sickness and the normal bumps, life became difficult. It is too easy to think that because things are going sideways in our life, then the joy that life should bring us is gone, and we become desperate. I don't know about you, but the news could depress me if I were to really take it into my spirit. *It is scary!*

What is the answer? What to do? Stop living, stop listening to the news, become lawless, become a recluse, run away? God has declared this answer to dwelling in safety.

> "The voice of JOY, and the voice of gladness,
> the voice of the bridegroom and the voice of the bride,
> the voice of them that shall say, Praise the Lord of hosts;
> for the Lord is good; for his mercy endures forever;
> and of them that shall bring the sacrifice of
> praise into the house of the LORD.
> For I will cause the captives of the land to
> return as at the first."
> —Jeremiah 33:11

The secret is to live in *His* presence. It is in *His* presence that joy comes, no matter the circumstances. I find that when Marion's joy disappears, and I begin to pray and thank *Him* for His goodness—by praising and worshiping Him, rather than focusing on the upheaval around me—that His joy that endured the cross for me takes over my innermost being, and my life attitude changes immediately.

Spread the news to everyone around us: Jesus' presence comes with *joy* in the midst of turmoil. The joy of the Lord is my strength. In *His* presence there is full joy!

Through the years of music history, the Song has been present. For believers to worship in song has always been God's plan because Jesus, God's son is the Song! The angels sang at His birth. Even under the Old Covenant, His presence was announced by praise; armies marched to the tunes of praise; songs proclaimed victory over enemies. Again and again, His Song is sung to the world. It has always been present and has been sung through all the generations— not always the same, but always there! When we sing to Him, He comes, and the Song is right there singing with us!

Why? Because the Song was in God's plan. The Song was in heaven with His Father. Lucifer was the original heavenly choir leader. Then he disobeyed, and God threw him out of heaven to the earth because of his disobedience. But God already had a plan. He also produced a substitute when Adam and Eve disobeyed Him. God was ready to put His plan into action. He covered their disobedience with skins of animals, because shedding innocent, living blood was required in His plan. God cast them out of the perfection of the Garden of Eden to wait for the appointed time. He later sent the real thing. Only perfect, sinless, living blood would bring about perfect, sinless, living forgiveness—total redemption from all sin.

John the Baptist declared it when Jesus appeared on the banks of the Jordan: "Behold! The Lamb of God who takes away the sin of the world!" (John 1:29).

The Song—God's perfect Lamb—was always present, before the world was ever created.

"Know that you were redeemed with the precious blood of
Christ, as of a lamb without blemish and without spot.
He indeed was foreordained before the foundation of the
world, but was manifest in these last time for you
who through Him believe in God,
who raised Him from the dead and gave Him glory,
so that your faith and hope are in God."
(1 Peter 1:18–21)

What are we going to be doing throughout all of the ages of eternity? We are going to be doing one thing: worshiping the Lamb. We are going to be worshiping the Lord Jesus Christ. Revelation Chapter Five tells it all. What is our song going to be? Let us take a look and find out. They had a scroll, a strong angel, and the Lion of the Tribe of Judah, the Root of David. Also some living creatures and elders falling face down before the Lamb that was slain from before the foundation of the world. Why? They had a song to sing. They had a message to give. They had something to declare. So listen, and even join in with them in their song of declaration. This is what they began to declare: "You are worthy, You are worthy, You are worthy."

When I get to heaven, it won't be, "Oh, God, please have the angels gather around me because I made so many trips to Africa, and I preached the gospel to so many people, and I saw so many souls saved. I'm God's man (or woman) of faith and power. Look—see what I have done. I'm the important one."

It will not be like that at all! That will be swept aside; it will no longer even matter. The only theme of eternity will be: "Worthy, Worthy, Worthy is the Lamb! You are Worthy, Lord Jesus, to receive all the glory and honor. You are the Lamb, slain from before the foundation of the world."

By the way, please do not wait to get to heaven to begin singing this song. Start singing now. We must raise our voices and sing our song with great gratitude and thanksgiving to the risen Christ our Redeemer, our Lord and soon coming King. It wouldn't do any harm to go back and take a fresh look at the Book again, and embrace with passion what the inspired word of God has to say. It would be powerful if we would begin talking to the Lord the way the men and women of the Bible talked to Him. Throughout the Scriptures, anyone who had a real meeting with God seemingly fell down prostrate on the ground. They began to bow down and worship and pray when they had an encounter with the living God. They did that down here on planet earth, because they knew that when they saw Him face to face, they could have only one response: to bow down, to worship Him, to magnify and exalt Him throughout all the ages of eternity.

The same Lamb was in the mind of God, was with God, and was God in eternity past—the Lamb who was, and is, and is to come. He was there; He is eternal; all things were made by Him, and for Him—long before time, as we understand it, began. He is the One who will be worshiped throughout all the ages of eternity. Those whom He has redeemed are going to begin to worship, magnify, and exalt Him, giving Him the glory, honor and praise throughout all eternity. It will be because of the Cross, because He is the Lamb of God. There is no other lamb. There is no other savior. He is the Lamb of God, and *He is God.*

"There is only one Lamb, Jesus the Christ.
Whatever we suffer cannot even be measured in comparison
to what He gave up when He came to be
God's Lamb and our Redeemer."
—Lewis Peterson, *It's Still the Cross*

As a ten-year-old girl I was exposed to awesome praise and worship. I remember laying in my bed listening to the congregation above me, praising and at the same time praying for revival. Dad had a hunger for the restoration of signs and wonders that the Bible talked about. The Lord had given a revelation to my father, which he taught to the congregation, and the result was powerful. It unified a split congregation. Even as a child, I was well aware that the Lord was beginning to do something very special.

This is how that happened. Before we left Ontario to move west, my Dad had received a letter asking him to preach revival meetings out west and share his testimony as a Spirit-filled Christian businessman. Dad decided to take a year off work to see what God wanted him to do.

He traveled to many churches sharing the message of the Gospel and was well accepted. Arriving at one of the churches, he found the pastor was very ill. The pastor's wife told him that since she was caring for her husband, he would have to take the service himself. Dad often told the story of trying to lead the singing himself. He called it a disaster, as he "couldn't hold a tune in a bucket." It just wasn't his calling. The spiritual climate in the church was hard as stone. After the service, Dad told the pastor's wife that he was going to spend the next day in fasting and prayer. It was a case of something had to happen, or he was going home.

During this time of seeking God, something powerful happened. Dad received a revelation of the sacrifice of praise. As he opened his Bible to the Psalms, his eyes fell on: "But thou art holy, O thou that inhabits the praises of Israel" (Psalm 22:3 KJV). The revelation was that God inhabits the praises of His people. He actually is enthroned (sits down) upon our praises! One does not have to feel anything to offer up a sacrifice of praise to God, because it was as stated: a sacrifice. If believers would give Him that Sacrifice of Praise He would respond to it by pouring out His Spirit. "Therefore by Him let us continually offer the Sacrifice of Praise to God, that is, the fruit of our lips, giving thanks to His name" (Hebrews 13:15).

That evening he preached what the Lord had shown him, then he instructed the people to stand and begin praising the Lord audibly in their own expression. The heavens opened, and the people entered into the presence of the Lord, experiencing a strong moving of the Holy Spirit. From that time on Dad never looked back from proclaiming what the Lord had revealed to him. Wherever he preached the message there would be praise and worship. As the years went on, he became known as the Apostle of Praise.

Worthy, O Worthy are you Lord,
Worthy to be thanked and praised and worshiped and adored.
Singing Hallelujah, Lamb upon the throne,
We worship and adore you. You make your glories known.

One of the miracles of healing that occurred at that time was during one of the services in Glad Tidings Church in Vancouver, BC. A young woman had been diagnosed with Leukemia and during the praise and worship service she fell to the floor. Everyone thought it was because of her illness and wanted to pick her up. Dad said, "No, it is the Lord," and we went on with the service. After the service was over she was still on the floor. Everyone else left, and we waited. Suddenly she opened her eyes and got up rejoicing, "I'm healed, I'm healed! We all were excited and my Dad said, "Go see your doctor tomorrow and see what he says." She did, and yes, there was no more cancer in her body—she lived into her 80s!

Another example was a prophetic word to a pregnant lady who was having problems. Dad prophesied that she would deliver twins, that she would go full term, and that they would both live. The mother and the twins are still alive and well.

Another time a very sedate businessman received the baptism of the Holy Spirit. He had been seeking the Holy Spirit for years, with no results. One Sunday after service he was there praying—such a faithful man. Suddenly he hit the floor and began to roll from one side of the church to the other. I had never seen a "holy roller" ever in my life. There was no doubt that the comforter had come!

For a season we had a young man living in our basement who was demon-possessed, and he would run away. I can remember my Dad running down the lane at the back of our house trying to catch him. Dad never gave up—deliverance had to come—and it did.

I learned early in my life that we don't live by His principles only, but by His presence. Even though I was raised on principle, and believe in it, when it comes to God, it is His presence that is the most important. Remember, we hide in God, and we dwell in His presence. He is my Lord! I run to Him by singing my praises to him. He is not just beside me; He dwells in me, and I in Him. He is my song!

"Do you know anything about an accordion?" I was asked. "No" I answered. "Well, here is one. I know you play the piano, and we need an accordion for the street meetings. Learn it." No questions asked—I did—and for years I played for both street meetings in Vancouver every week. I played and sang and gave my testimony, and Lew was the bouncer and sang and preached. The street meetings in the inner city produced lots of excitement.

We also helped in the outreach missions. Lew preached and I helped with giving out the food. It was rather challenging. One time after Lew had preached, the person in charge of the mission told my Dad how well Lew had preached. Next time Dad saw Lew, he asked, "Well how did the mission meeting go on Saturday?"

"Really well. I preached."

Dad looked surprised, and said, "You preached?"

"Yes, men came to pray afterwards. The leaders thought I did okay."

Dad answered, "Even if I was a drunk, I wouldn't listen to a young whipper-snapper like you." Dad was like that. He didn't believe in encouragement, let alone flattery. But I guess there was some truth in what he said—after all, Lew was only seventeen years old!

A friend said to Lew, "Come with me. I am going to canvas the area for kids and start a Sunday School in the Mission. Want to help?" And to me he said, "How 'bout you?"

"Sure, I will play the piano and I can teach," I replied. This was how I began ministering outside the church walls. We were part of that Sunday School for years, and it finally became a church that is still in existence many years later.

One of the things Lew and his buddies liked to do was spend time on the downtown streets witnessing. Other witnesses would just stand around with their magazines held up, trying to get people to stop and talk. The guys would go stand beside them and hold up their open Bibles. That sure cleared the streets!

We learned to preach in a youth gathering called "Wells of Joy." We met on Sunday afternoons before the street meeting and evening service. It was our time to learn to lead worship, sing specials, prophecy, follow the Spirit, exhort, and sometimes preach. We all had our turn to be the leader of the service. The church building had an unused third floor, so Dad allowed us to clean it out, decorate it, and use it as our youth room.

While we had our service, Dad was conducting an open preaching "Body Ministry" time for the would-be adult preachers. That time was very popular. Each would-be preacher had seven minutes to have his say. The would-be preachers would line up to have their opportunity and even raced each other to get up to the pulpit first. Dad would sit in the front row and listen. It looked like he was asleep, but he wasn't, and you would find that out when he got up to publically critique everyone.

We also had Pioneer Girls and Boys Brigade clubs, where we started out being the kids and ended up joining the leaders as we got older. By the time Lew and I were seventeen we were leading.

We were the youngest teens in Canada to finish their qualifications and become leaders, and we both taught Sunday School as well. We enjoyed very full years as teens. Not by programs, although we had them, but we were in love with Jesus, and He was the center of our lives.

I loved singing in the choir. I am a worshiper, and that is what God is looking for in my spirit. Worship comes from the heart. Worship is universal, because it is heart. Different methods of worship must be expressions of the heart—not a show of talent. It is not how good you are, but how your heart is worshiping your Lord. You become good at what you do, because you want to bring glory to Him.

I learned to worship and praise everywhere and anywhere. Out loud when appropriate, in my head when not, but continually. Singing in my head is the best way to get to sleep—so much better that counting sheep. Sometimes I would wake up singing an old hymn that I had learned for my Music Badge in Pioneer Girls. The song had been with me all night.

At one of our youth camps we invited Pastor Laurie from Edmonton to come and be our speaker. He is the pastor of Peoples Church, which began during the "Jesus Movement" and is still going strong today with an assortment of international members. At camp that year he taught on the Lordship of Jesus Christ. It was a powerful message and, when received by the Holy Spirit, changed the lives of the young people. We all went home quoting his challenges: "If He is not Lord of all, he is not Lord at all," and, "Compromise brings failure." He taught us to state at any opportunity, answering a question, answering the phone, any greeting or good bye: "Jesus is Lord." Every one of us—leaders and campers alike—came home challenged and fired up.

Sometimes we become saturated with all that is going on around us daily, and we can lose our closeness to Him. This happened to us on more than one occasion. Lew and I were going through a dry time, feeling some discouragement along with a bit of frustration and disappointment. One afternoon when Lew was out doing church visitation, he heard a new song on the car radio that expressed how he felt. He came bursting into our office, bubbling over, "You have to hear this song! It is just for us." On the way home we went to the bookstore, found the new release, and when we got home we played it over and over again, letting The Song minister to us. It became our prayer. We had to learn that it wasn't the music, the words, the talent, or even the desire. It was the "Heart of Worship" that mattered. It is all about Him, not me, or what method I use to worship. It is my heart in my worshipping that gives Him a throne to sit upon and sing with me.

Actually, because we dwell with Him at all times, He has given us the way to be continually attached. This, I believe, is the secret. There are four ways to remain in His presence 24/7. My life has been one of prayer, continually praying for people I see, or meet, or read about. On and on, I just keep praying, asking, believing, instead of getting disgruntled. It has been work, but I accomplish it more than I did last year or ten years back. I'm working on it!

"Let my prayer be set before you as incense
and the lifting of my hands as the evening sacrifice."
—Psalm 141:2

"But you, Beloved, building yourselves up on your most holy
faith praying in the Holy Spirit."
—Jude 20

My favorite way to pray is in the Spirit. I love to drive down the road in my car, praying in the Spirit out loud. Many times I don't know what I am praying for, but He does. I am a very thankful person, so this makes it a little easier. Be thankful for what He has done for us, or what someone else has done. I thank him for a close parking spot on a cold rainy day. I thank him for a good meal and a good night's sleep. There is so much to be thankful for. He has done so much for me. "Let us come before His presence with thanksgiving" (Psalm 95:2).

I love to be in His presence, so I look for things to be thankful for. Sometimes I get a funny look, because the person wonders why I am thanking them. I have a big reason! Praise Him for all he has done.

"Praise Him for His mighty acts,
Praise Him according to His excellent greatness.
Let everything that has breath, Praise the Lord!
Praise Ye The Lord."
—Psalm 150

It is called the Sacrifice of Praise, but there are so many way to express my praise that it really isn't that difficult. Sacrifice means I really don't want to, but I really don't have a choice. I do it anyway— it is a command!

I worship God because He is God. If He never did another thing for me, it doesn't matter. I would worship Him always, because of Who He is. That's it. "Worship God!" (Revelation 22:9).

I like to bow before Him, and worship makes me feel humbled. Imagine being accepted to worship the God of the universe, the Lord of all. He created me, I am made of His dirt, but he wants me to worship Him! I can't wrap my mind around that, but it is a fact, and still I may worship Him.

He is Lord, He is Lord.
He is risen from the dead, and He is Lord.
Every knee shall bow, and every tongue confess
That Jesus Christ is Lord.
—Anonymous

In September 2018 I was in Uganda once again for six weeks. Since moving back to the west 20 years earlier, Lew and I had been there to visit a few more times. My Lord went before me and met me there. My first Sunday was in Life Church (formerly RUN Bible Church) and I had a blast! My, how they can praise and worship. I greeted the people, many of whom didn't know me, as the church has grown so much. It was a great reunion as I talked about my beginning dreams of ministry in Africa, specifically Uganda. I felt their love, and I love them in return.

My second Sunday was in Kawuyu. I dedicated two babies. One mother was named Marion, and one of the babies was Marion! Standing at the pulpit, I was afraid! I had prepared sufficiently, and I had a word, but what if I couldn't articulate my thoughts properly? What if the anointing wasn't there any more? I was back with my people in Uganda, and they were expecting me to have a word for them. This had been my place, in my time—a chapel on the Institute property, and now a growing Church in Kawuku, on the road to Entebbe. I began to speak and introduced my traveling companion, Shirley. I said hello to the congregation, most of whom after 20 years hadn't met me, but had heard about Pastor Marion. I opened my Bible and began to read and share my heart.

Something inside me burst. Like a bubble coming up from the bottom of the well, it rose, and I wondered if I was going to burst. I looked down at Pastor Ken and Shirley. Ken had a huge smile and Shirley was giggling, hand over her mouth. They felt it too. My Lord was there, and after ten years of drought, I felt it.

The preaching came back with a vengeance, bursting out of my mouth. I was no longer afraid it was gone! His presence was responding to my broken heart and healing me. I knew I was being released, renewed and restored. It was amazing. In a moment of time, there it was—so wonderful to be free! He had not forsaken me. I was not on the shelf, and He hadn't changed His mind. His calling was without repentance. Thank You, My Lord Jesus.

The next Sunday was in Wakiso. Pastor Emmanuel is a strong leader of this church that he pioneered. Emmanuel grew up at the Institute property where his father had worked for us, and the boys would play church. He was always the preacher, and now his people consider him to be his people's Apostle. He oversees other churches and is a powerful man of God. The singing, the rejoicing, the life in that place was overwhelming. Years ago in their play church, his brother Ammoni led the singing. He loved Jesus with all his heart, but was handicapped in his expressions of worship. As we were singing and rejoicing in the service, I saw a man come dancing up the isle onto the platform, where the choir was praising and leading the worship. I watched this man worship with tears streaming down his face, as he loved on Jesus. It was Ammoni! I began to weep. I couldn't believe it. There was no indication of his handicap. Oh, how he worshiped! Shirley couldn't believe it when I told her about his childhood. Obviously, he was healed in his worship. What a day that was as we rejoiced in seeing one another again—now grown up and serving the Lord together.

Next Sunday in Kawempe, I was with Pastor Edward. I have known him since he was a boy in the church, way back when Pastor Agatha was his pastor. After I finished preaching, Edward asked me to pray for his lead musician, so I asked him to come to me. That same bubble climbed up to my mouth and the prophetic flowed. While I was praying for him, the pastor asked all the musicians and the leadership team to come, and he asked me to pray with them. These were very precious moments, as I had the opportunity to pray a prophetic prayer over them. I was so blessed, and I was aware of My Lord right there with me. Amazing! Restoration is an awesome experience when you are the one who needs to be restored!

In the prayer time after the service, folk were filled with the Holy Spirit or refreshed in the consciousness of the presence of God. I love to pray with people to be filled with the Spirit, and that unction was restored to me again. I am blessed! His Grace is sufficient.

My final Sunday was in Life Church in Kampala. It was the 30th Anniversary of the beginning of RUN Bible Church and Ministries, now known as Life Church. The presence of the Lord was electric. Everyone sat on the edge of their seat with expectation, and they were not disappointed. The theme was the future: "Dream Again." With everything in me, I preached my burden for Life Church. "It is time for you to work (act) oh Lord, for they have regarded your law as void!" (Psalm 119:26). He continues to work, building His kingdom and maturing His bride. He still has a plan to be finished. Habakkuk 2:2, 3 defines how progress happens:

- Appointed time
- It will speak
- Wait – patience doing its perfect work
- It will come
- It will not tarry

> "Brethren, I do not count myself to have apprehended:
> but one thing I do; forgetting those things which are behind
> and reaching forward to those things which are ahead,
> I press toward the mark of the high calling of God
> in Christ Jesus."
> —Philippians 3:13, 14

Pastor Richard closed the celebration with the future look for Life Church. I rejoice in the plans the Lord has for our Ugandan family as they continue on in their journey.

In those six weeks we worked hard. We attended and spoke at numerous meetings and had a wonderful and fulfilling time. We were scheduled to be busy in meetings or visiting every day. Certainly we were not bored. My Lord was with us every step of the way. His grace was overwhelming as He undergirded us daily. The traffic was unbelievable, the roads indescribable, but the church is great—alive and well!

I know that wherever I am, and whomever I am with, He is there: Immanuel, "God with us." Although there are difficult, overwhelming times and languages differences, He is there. I couldn't imagine being in Uganda without Lew, but I went and found My Lord was there waiting for me! I also was reminded that He is the Lord of all the earth, and those folk know Him and love Him just as I do. He is their Lord as well as my Lord! Mukama Mulungi!

Jesus freely, joyfully sacrificed his life for the world. He became the supreme sacrifice. He died and was buried. But . . . He rose again, demonstrating His power to share His eternal life with the human race, once and for all. It Is Finished! No more need for any other blood to be sacrificed, or any other life to be taken to cover man's sins. This is the power of redemptive Grace! It is free – eternal life for the believing. He forgave all of us all of our sins in order that we can live forever with him. Just believe it!

> "For God so loved the world that He gave
> His only begotten son that whoever believes in Him shall not
> perish but have everlasting life."
> —John 3:16

His birth was announced by heaven. "For there is born to you this day in the city of David a Savior, who is Christ the Lord. Suddenly there was with the angel a multitude of the heavenly host praising God saying: 'Glory to God in the Highest, and on earth peace, goodwill toward men!'" (Luke 2:11–14).

His resurrection was confirmed by heaven. Early on the first day of the week . . . women came to the tomb. They found the stone rolled away, they entered the tomb and did not find the body of Jesus. They were greatly perplexed, and then they saw two men in shining garments standing by. They were alarmed and one said: "You seek Jesus of Nazareth, who was crucified. Why do you seek the living among the dead? He is not here, He is risen!" (Mark 16:6; Luke 24:5–6).

> "If Christ is not risen, your faith is futile;
> you are still in your sins.
> But Christ is risen from the dead.
> For as in Adam all die,
> so in Christ all shall be made alive."
> —1 Corinthians 15;17, 20, 22

The Disciples were with Jesus 40 days, and then—while they watched—He was taken up to heaven, and those two men in shining garments appeared again!

" . . . This same Jesus, who was taken up from
you into heaven,
will so come in like manner as you saw
Him go into heaven."
—Acts 1:11

What grace! What power! His redemptive grace! His saving, redeeming power! Every possession incorporated in His Name belongs to us, through his sacrifice and His resurrection life. How amazing. All we believers have to do is believe and act, by faith in Him, upon that provision. It is already ours.

"But we see Jesus, who was made a little lower that the angels,
for the suffering of death crowned with glory and honor,
that He, by the grace of God, might taste death for everyone."
—Hebrews 2:9

"Having boldness to enter the Holiest by the blood of Jesus,
by a new and living way which He consecrated for us."
—Hebrews 10:19, 20

"For I am not ashamed of the gospel if Christ,
for it is the power of God to salvation
for everyone who believes."
—Romans1:16

I want to conclude this chapter with the testimony of the man who passed on to us the revelation of true worship and how to experience it. "But you are Holy, enthroned upon the praises of Israel" (Psalm 22:3).

The Last Will and Testament of Reg Layzell

"I commit with humble reverence my soul into the hands of my Savior, the Lord Jesus Christ, with full confidence that having redeemed it and washed it in His most precious blood, He will present it faultless before the throne of my Heavenly Father. I entreat my family to maintain and defend at all hazard and at any cost or personal sacrifice, the blessed doctrine of the complete atonement for sin through the blood of Jesus Christ once offered and through that alone."

Wonderful, Wonderful Jesus,
He is my friend, true to the end.
He gave Himself to redeem me,
Jesus, Wonderful Lord.

Right: Abbotsford

Below: Marion at the Piano, Gospel Mission to Uganda

Right: Botswana

Above: Church Choir, Uganda

Right: Lew in Church, Kenya

Left: Taiwan

Right: Bwerenga

Left: Ghana

Right: RUN Bible Church, Kampala, Uganda

Left: Mwanza, Tanzania

CHAPTER TWO

"I Do"

O ur years of sorting this romance thing out had taken us a lifetime! I can't say we totally did figure it out, but I do know it was a great adventure as it developed throughout the years. Here are my memories of our youth and a 65-year romance.

It was 1952. Lew's heart was beating erratically and his mind was racing, thinking wonderful thoughts. There she was, right there in front of him wearing a soft green dress with a matching headpiece. Her long blonde hair shone in the light as she was playing her cello in the church orchestra. *She is so beautiful! I will marry her someday! What if she doesn't love me too? Then what will I do? How will I manage when I have to get past her Dad, my Pastor? What will my friends say? My Parents?*

Through the years I had heard Lew tell this story over and over again. At the time Lew was 14 and I was 13. I had just been a junior bridesmaid in a wedding and was wearing my bridesmaid dress and a hat—really? We were part of the youth group in our home church, and yes—my Dad was the pastor, a man to be respected and feared! I didn't know Lew at all, and he was already working in the family masonry business, way beyond my reach as a friend. I was a schoolgirl; he had a job. He was a big guy, mature, and already a leader in the youth group. I really hadn't given him any thought.

Don't get me wrong. I liked the boys and welcomed their friendship. In fact, from the time I was old enough to notice the male gender (supposedly within the church youth group—that was the expectation), I was never without a "boyfriend." But Lew Peterson was not on my radar.

Lew worked fast, and by the time I had turned 14 we were "going steady." We could not date, because by our standards the youth group did everything together. We rode the city busses, climbed the Vancouver, BC mountains, swam the Pacific, worshiped together, and celebrated with parties at the church. We played softball, had youth camp, enjoyed boys and girls clubs, and most of us had "boyfriends" within the group. Those were wonderful years.

Years later Lew told our daughter Mari Lou, "So many of the boys had a crush on your mom, but I won!"

The chemistry affection between a boy and a girl is an interesting subject. Our "romance" began as fun with the group. Our parents depended on the security of group activity—knowing where we were and who we were with. We were not angels, and we broke the ranks from time to time. There really wasn't much opportunity for that, but we managed!

There was safety in numbers, so no one tattled on the others. We were loyal to each other, but we had our "moments." One such moment might be a sitting in front of your boyfriend in church and touching feet during an hour-long sermon. We would hold hands and sneak a kiss once in a while when out with the group, if no supervisor was around. But fortunately we had guidelines and a healthy fear of God (and the Pastor) that kept us on a somewhat straight and narrow path.

Thank God, He was watching over us. "His eye is on the sparrow," and I know he was watching over us! We had all the emotions, and with the chemistry there from the very start, we knew it had to be controlled. Thank God for that. It also made for a good marriage.

We desperately worked at being true disciples of Jesus in spite of our fleshly weaknesses.

> *In the name of Jesus, in the name of Jesus,*
> *We have the Victory.*
> *In the name of Jesus, in the name of Jesus*
> *Demons will have to flee.*
> *When we stand on the name of Jesus*
> *Tell me who can stand against us?*
> *In the name of Jesus, Jesus we have the victory.*

Lew was working up the street from our house. Dad and Mom were away and Pastor and Sis Schoch were looking after the Church, as well as my sister Ruth and me. I snuck away to see Lew. Not a very smart move. Anyway, Lew had come down off the roof and we were together in the basement sneaking a kiss, when I heard a voice: "Marion, Lew, are you down there?" We just about died. The Prophet had found us. God had spoken to him! He was laughing at us as we came out to the street. We didn't realize Dave Schoch used to be a plumber, so when the little kids told him where I had gone, all he did was look for a construction site! We were humiliated and knew we would "get it" when Dad got home, but to our surprise, nothing happened—whew!

Lew spent most of his time off working at our house, with my Mom supervising. Mom was an angel. She loved Lew. She so enjoyed having him around, and he could do no wrong. He had made an agreement with Dad to do seven jobs around our house, the equivalent to Jacob's (Old Testament) service for Rachel. The problem was that within a year's time, Dad owed Lew some years. Since we were very young teens, and had a lot of maturing to do, I am thankful that Dad didn't discourage our friendship. He just closely supervised it.

Looking back on 65 years of "going steady" (including 59 years of marriage, while being youth, assistant, or lead pastors), I have made a few observations concerning the romantic side of man-woman relationships:

1. Quickly is not the rule; it is the exception.
2. Age is not an automatic issue. Principle and necessary development is what is important.
3. And foremost: Have both shown their love for God and the desire to serve Him all the days of their lives?

Thinking back on our years of Pastoral Counseling, Lew and I developed a pattern to help young people choose their lifelong partners and enjoy a romance to be remembered with joy, and not regret.

- **Stage 1 — Attraction**
  Physical, attitude to life, similar enjoyments, language, home life.

- **Stage 2 – Friendship**
  Best friends: you are an item; do things together; common friends; respect and loyalty for each other; understanding reactions to situations. This is probably the longest stage, building a foundation for the future.

- **Stage 3 – Love and Relationship**
  Emotions; chemistry; togetherness; honesty; self-control; background. Where are we going with this? Open discussions about differences and expectations.

- **Stage 4 – Courtship**
  Practical reasoning; protection; careful not to offend; goals; future desires; children? Parents and family; money matters; Pastoral marriage counseling; engagement; plans and more plans.

- **Stage 5 – Marriage**
  Covenant for life; sex

Marriage is a covenant made before God, family and witnesses, like His covenant of Grace with us at salvation. God is the founder of every aspect of a marriage. He originated marriage. Love needs to be present, because we are created in God's image, and God is Love. When pledged together in the marriage covenant before Him, we become witnesses of His perfect picture of Christ and the Church, the Bride and Bridegroom, so much in love.

We were very serious in our covenant of marriage. We determined that divorce would never be in our vocabulary. Good or bad, we would always honor our covenant before God, our family, friends and the congregation. We soon discovered that even though we made the covenant and had a deep love for each other, *Marriage is work!* After some early "hick-ups" we purposed to tell each other sincerely, "I love you," every day. This was our declaration whether we felt like it or not, and we sealed it with a covenant kiss. It wasn't always easy.

Did we have disagreements? Of course! Hurts? Yes, those too. But at the end of Lew's life, as I was his caregiver, I wept buckets of tears knowing that it was worth all the struggles. He was my man, and I loved him so deeply!

Lew's words of counsel were, "In marriage, if there are no disagreements, then one person is not necessary!" We didn't look for troubles. They just happened, but we were ready to talk them out, come to a decision, and then act together on it. We had many strong discussions, since we were both strong leaders and very opinionated, but we worked at not letting that disrupt the responsibility to maintain our love and marriage. It worked for 59 years!

We celebrated 63 Christmases together. Lew loved to tell everyone that at age 17 he was introduced to the Layzell style of a formally set table. He said he was afraid to pick up the crystal, because his bricklayer hands were so big and strong that he would break the goblet. Dad always came to the table in a formal dinner jacket. As the Christmases went by, Lew became accustomed to the English formality and actually enjoyed the display of elegance.

Engagement

Eventually, after we had been 'going steady' for five years, Lew made his trip into Dad's office to ask if we could become officially engaged. Talk about shredded nerves! I so wanted to wear that ring! When he asked Dad, the answer was, "You will have to wait till she is 18."

Lew replied, "Okay."

When Lew came into the church lobby where I was waiting, I asked, "What did he say?"

"You will have to wait till she is 18."

I was shocked! "I am 18! What did you say?"

"Okay."

Through the years Lew told that story many times, and we never did ask Dad if he really didn't know how old I was, or if he was just seeing how long it would take for Lew to come back! A few weeks later Lew made another appointment, went into the "inner sanctum" and asked again. Permission was granted and I had my ring. I was officially engaged to Lewis Edward Peterson. We waited for one more year to get married."

Dad's control began to soften in our courtship year. Our times alone had been very few, and always chaperoned by my sister Ruth. Lew always said that Ruth never married because she was always with us, and never had the opportunity to find a husband. Lew's job included working at Keats Island, where Dad owned a summer cottage. On one of our trips back from the cottage, we were driving through Stanley Park. Dad was behind us in his car and signaled us to stop. He came to the driver's-side window, and Lew rolled it down. Dad said, "I see a car ahead with a two-headed driver." Yep, that was us! Dad handed him a newspaper and said, "Put this between you."

"I Do"

We were married in the midst of a revival, so weddings were very simple. In spite of all the rules and regulations that my Dad thought were required to keep the wedding spiritual in such carnal situations, (my Mom & Dad had eloped), we did have a good wedding. We were married in our weekly Friday evening service, with not too much hoopla, and not exactly what I wanted, but Mother begged on my behalf. Our wedding was on Valentine's Day, February 14, 1958.

Red is one of my favorite colors—bright and exciting—so I requested a red and white wedding.

"Definitely not!" was Dad's answer to that, so I settled for coral and blue.

I wanted my girlfriends to be bridesmaids.

"If you want a bridesmaid, then it has to be your sister." I was not friends with my sister.

"You can have the secretary as a bridesmaid, if you really need to have two bridesmaids."

She was living with us at the time and was like another daughter—so that was that!

My dress was classic and beautiful, a white brocade with Chantilly lace that we bought at the Army & Navy store for $13. I borrowed a shoulder-length veil, tucked into a simple tiara from a school friend. My Aunt Marion sent me a blue garter, and I was set. Lew chose his brother and the secretary's brother, who also lived with us, to be his groomsmen, and the church looked after everything else. Lew and I walked down the aisle together, as Dad didn't see the purpose of doing that himself! Dad married us. We knelt, and when he had finished praying for us we stood. Stepping over the kneeling cushions, Dad kissed me on the cheek and said, "Now you can do as you like." Lew never did kiss his bride (at the wedding)!

You're Blended Splendid

We had a nice reception. They set up the platform with the head table and a beautiful wedding cake, served sandwiches, sweets, and of course, ice cream cups with wood spoons. All was well. The entire congregation (over 500 people) was invited and they were all there. We received so many gifts and cards. Six of them were identical and said, "You're blended splendid."

It was obvious that as the congregation watched us grow up they knew this was a good blend. We were either preaching in the inner city mission, teaching Sunday School, in street meetings, teaching Kid's Club, singing in the choir, playing the piano and accordion, or leading worship. Yes, the Lord helped us to lay the "best friend" foundation first, and together we worked at the blending process. We knew marriage was not 50/50, but we were each 100% individuals, and it was important to blend our lives in every way.

Dad did not make our blending easy, and my High School graduation had been one of those times. It was on a Friday night, and that was church night, so Dad would not come. I felt I always fell short of pleasing him, so I wanted him to be proud of me and my accomplishments. He allowed Mom to come and gave Lew a special dispensation to miss the Friday Night Service. We Christian kids at school had an after party. Lew and I went, but I had to be home by 11:00. We rushed away from the party, arriving home at 11:05. As we came up the stairs the door opened and Dad said, "Isn't it time you were going home, young man?" Not, "How did it go?" or any other conversation. I had done well in school and was very disappointed. It took me many years to forgive Dad's attitude that evening.

The Chase

Now we were married, and it was time to get on with the life we had dreamed about. But first, our friends had plans. After the reception, our wonderful friends chased us for two hours around the city, giving us a scary time! It was amazing. Here I was on the floor of the back seat, in my going away outfit—hat and all—covered by a blanket, with Lew hunched over me trying to stay out of sight. We ended up in a ditch. Our pursuers pulled us out of the ditch, and off they went again, chasing us as we went racing around Richmond. Looking back, I really think our driver and the pursuers were in this plan together. Anyway, we finally escaped in one piece into the gated New Westminster bus depot, and grabbed the safety of our own car that we had parked there so no one would mess with it.

The Honeymoon

That night we made it over the USA border to Bellingham for our first night. The next day we went on to visit Bill and Evelyn Hamon in Toppinish,WA, then continued south to Disneyland, visited David Schoch in Long Beach, and on into Mexico for our two-week honeymoon.

While in Long Beach, Lew turned 21 on February 27th. Dave was so much fun and teased us unmercifully. After we celebrated Lew's birthday, Dave took us to Knott's Berry Farm. I was a protected young woman, totally ignorant and naïve. Dave sent me to look at an old cowboy statue sitting in the two-seater outhouse. The statue said to me, "Come on in Marion, there are seats for two." I didn't know what to say, I was so embarrassed! I turned to see David and Lew laughing at me. David had given my name to a controller in another building, who told it to the old cowboy by earpiece.

We had a wonderful, very joyful time. On the way home we stopped in Sacramento to preach for Joe Morse, who had advertized Lew as "Squeek'n Peterson". Joe was a wonderful friend and a natural clown. Before salvation he had been a professional clown and had lived the high life. He was crazy! One day we were driving around Sacramento with him. He stopped the car in the downtown. "See that building over there? That is the old Ohambra Theater. I am going to buy it for my church." He grabbed my hand and got out of the car. "Come on Lew, every time I go by here I go and lay hands on that building and claim it in Jesus' name for my church!"

So that is exactly what we did. There in downtown Sacramento we laid hands on that building and prayed in front of God and everybody. God is the provider, and in later years Joe owned that building. It became his building, housing his Jesus People congregation. While we were pastoring in Yuba City, Lew preached for Joe many times in that building.

True Love

As I remember our adventures and try to record them, my heart is so thankful for God's goodness in giving me such a wonderful, honest, romantic man, who literally and happily dragged me around the world in order to be true to God's purpose and destiny for our lives.

My Dad was old school. Encouragement was flattery; demonstrations of affection were for women; men showed their love by provision, leading and keeping their families in proper order. As I became a teen and began to understand the possibility of demonstrated human love between a man and a woman, and I felt my mother's longing for affection and honor, I hurt with her!

I didn't understand the closeness of family love and certainly not a Father's emotional love. In my Father's love, I experienced care, yes; provision, yes; guidance, yes. In my head I knew Dad's concept of love, but something was missing for my Mom. I wanted to find out what that was.

When Lew came into my life, I began to feel something different about him, and I liked it. As our love developed, for the first time I understood how a man's love was different. As something that a woman longed for, it could be emotional, satisfying and deep. That is where I wanted to live the rest of my life. I felt that love in myself and also wanted to experience it toward me, from my husband. When we married, I did. Now after 61 years, as I write this on February 14, 2019, that romantic feeling of love for Lew has not diminished. He was certainly a romantic. The demonstration of his love for me was clear in every way, and I remember it to this day.

Categorically, I must be clear: the act of sex is *neither love, nor romance, nor marriage*. It is simply a feeling, and an action we call "sex" (not a Biblical term), originating in carnal, fleshly desires. It is simply the sexual act, nothing more. Outside of marriage, God calls it lust, adultery, fornication, and sin. Extramarital sex is disobedience and defames God's character. The result destroys lives, homes, and nations. God created the sexual act naturally, within every living thing he created, for procreation purposes only.

At creation, God changed the pattern when he created Adam and Eve. Of all God's creatures, humans are the only ones made *in His image*. On the sixth day God created Adam in His image, so that had to have meant *with love*. When Adam felt that something was missing, God took a piece out of Adam and created Eve. Now Adam and Eve together could "replenish the earth" and because they possessed the love part of God, it made the process thrilling! We cannot "make" love. God is already love. Love already is! God gave His love to us to enjoy. For the actions of a man and a woman to be love, first they must make a covenant (an unbreakable commitment) of marriage, sealing their covenant with God's love, which was created in them in the first place. To this they add a token of the promise (a ring), and folk to witness the covenant (family and friends). The feelings, the chemistry, and the romance come first, then the marriage and the consummating of God's love. Couples then enjoy all the wonderful feelings of satisfied love God's way, and sometimes they are blessed with children. "Cleaving with the feeling" is true love.

Lew firmly believed Paul's admonitions:

"Husbands, love your wives,
even as Christ also loved the church, and gave himself for it."
—Ephesians 5:25

"Therefore a man shall leave his father and
mother and cleave to his wife,
and they shall become one flesh."
—Genesis 2:24

Lew was my best friend, my confidant, my husband, my lover—a romantic, a caregiver, my provider, my security, my partner-in-crime, and my lifelong Pastor. Yes, Jesus was all of those first, but Lew was His human demonstration to me, and I will forever be grateful. He understood the principle of the sacrifice Jesus made as the Father's Son to his Bride, The Church. As a husband he put those principles into practice, respecting me and preferring me above himself continuously. Discussions with other women have caused me to understand that I was probably a bit spoiled.

Romance is God's idea. He wants his Son to romance the church, His bride. Jesus loves us so deeply that He obeyed His Father and laid down His life for His love. That is you and me, and all we have to do is let Him romance us. All the accounts of the generations in the Bible that we gloss over when reading them are real love stories, meaning someone loving someone, and in that love, making another human being and beginning a new generation. Isn't it wonderful that God made the love experience to be enjoyable, pleasant and exciting. Enjoy your love God's way, for *God is love.*

"Marriage is honorable among all and the bed undefiled."
—Hebrews 13:4

The Bible is full of love stories: God's love for us, Ruth and Boaz, Abraham and Sarah, Jacob and Rachael, the Song of Solomon, Hosea, and many more. I'm amused at the record of Isaac and Rebecca's love affair. "One day, after they had been there quite a long time, Abimelech, king of the Philistines, looked out his window and saw Isaac fondling his wife Rebekah. Abimelech sent for Isaac and said, "So she's your wife. Why did you tell us, 'She is my sister'?" (Genesis 26:8, 9).

Even the ungodly king recognized God's principle that the intimacy of romance belongs in the covenant of marriage.

"Unless the Lord builds the house,
they labor in vain who build it;

Unless the Lord guards the city,
the watchman stays awake in vain."
—Psalm 127:1

Ugandan Marriages

In biblical times, arranged marriages were the custom. More recently, in various eastern countries arranged marriages are still the custom. Some are good, and some are bad. But I have observed that even with our western customs, some are good, and some are bad.

In Uganda that was the custom until recent years, and it still is in some rural areas. In the educated world, nowadays most parents allow their offspring to choose their mate, with approval according to the clan's and the family's status, and in the case of believers, a common church. Parents' choices were based upon family equality, heritage, status, education, age—really no different than in the West. My parents wanted my choice to be someone who would look after me, was caring, could supply my needs, and, because of my strong faith, someone who had the same faith.

Nowadays, I think the greatest challenge is how to bring the combination of East and West together. When students go abroad for education they experience a different approach to courtship, wedding and marriage, then return to their homes where in some cases the old traditions are disappearing. We in the West hear about the different customs, and without understanding we often criticize. But it is not really different, it is just a *different way* of doing the same thing. In Africa, when it comes to weddings, the influence of the West has been both good and bad.

Just like in the West, some new couples don't want all the fuss and expense, because they have to pay for their own wedding, so customs are changing with the times. If a Ugandan couple wants their wedding to be simple, the worry is, *what will the extended family think?*

Some Ugandan traditions are much like the West, just carried out in a different way. One, called the Introduction, is the same as an Engagement Party, only with a different approach. In today's reality they are done in fun and tradition, not in reality. I always enjoyed attending them. In the old tradition it was the time for introducing the suitor to the young lady who was ready for marriage. The father and the suitor agreed on the dowry, and then the couple would meet for the Introduction. The young woman did not have any choice, but if she had objections she could express herself, and the outcome would depend on her relationship with her father. Usually she would agree, and the arrangements would continue. The dowry offered indicated her value, and in Ugandan tradition it would probably be a cow or two! All the arrangements were discussed, and the acceptance approved, at this Introduction.

In Uganda in today's world, the couple have already agreed themselves and done some courting. They have met the each other's parents, and all the plans are agreed upon between them privately. So the Introduction is more like a nod to tradition. I remember one that I attended. The young lady had her friends all around, with some older ladies there as the "Aunts," who traditionally advise the young lady as the negotiations are discussed. But on this day they were just acting out the old tradition.

The suitor came with bags of rice and sugar, then kerosene, baskets of fresh vegetables, and a live goat to reinforce his request. Then they began to dicker. Each side had a representative spokesman, and they went at it. What a hilarious drama! So much chatter and laughing. Then it was settled, and everyone was pleased. The date for the wedding was set (of course it had already been agreed upon). The bride price or dowry (also already agreed upon) was a coffee table. All went home happy, and the bride's parents received all that was necessary for the suitor to have his bride. Interestingly enough, the coffee table was made and given to the parents, and then on their wedding it was given back to the couple for their home. What a big change from tradition.

In the West the bride receives the gifts, but in the East the parents get the gifts. Nowadays the girls would like an engagement ring, so the West shows itself again along with the dress, the tiara, the veil, etc. The wedding rental business is strong, because purchasing the clothing just isn't practical or affordable. The reception is usually a feast, but the cutting of the cake is another western fashion. Elaborate honeymoons are unusual. Most new couples usually will visit extended family or friends not far away. East and West are certainly meeting when it comes to courtship, weddings and marriage. Tradition is strong, and followed respectfully, but in actuality each couple chooses according to their financial status and their church affiliation.

I know not why God's wondrous grace
to me He has made known,
Nor why unworthy Christ in love
redeemed me for His own,
I know not how this saving faith to me He did impart,
Nor how believing in His word, wrought
peace within my heart
But I know whom I have believed, and am
persuaded that He is able
To keep that which I've committed unto
Him against that day.
—*Daniel Webster Whittle / James McGranahan (1883)*

Anniversaries

We celebrated all our wedding anniversaries every year. I don't remember where or how we celebrated each one, but we loved to remember our beginnings and how good the Lord had been to us each year. We celebrated in Mombasa, Vancouver, Calgary, Kampala, Olympia, Sacramento, Portland, Victoria, Cruising thru the Panama Canal, and more.

We celebrated our first anniversary with Dave and Fran Huebert in Chinatown, Vancouver. They had been married on February 7th and we were married a week later on the 14th. We had to be at church in Vancouver on Friday evening. Dave and Fran were patient with our rules, but the service went late, so our celebration was late, and we were hungry and cranky. In those days you didn't miss church for any reason, except your own funeral, according to my Dad's rule. However, we enjoyed ourselves, and the meal. We had been pastoring in Abbotsford just a few months, and Dave and Fran were in the congregation. This is when our longtime friendship began.

On our 25th anniversary Mari Lou put together a celebration in Yuba City. It was time for the Revival Fellowship Conference. That year it was in Sacramento, so she arranged for all our ministry friends to come to the party. It was wonderful, and everyone was there. Pastor Schoch re-married us, Dad made his speech, and we cut the cake again. This time we kissed at the ceremony in front of God and everybody. As Dave Schoch was renewing our vows with us, with great glee he told the story. It was the first my Dad had even heard about it—talk about sweet protection. But it was too late to be grounded.

For our anniversary trip I wanted to go to Hawaii. One of the girls in the Yuba City Church was familiar with Maui and knew of a good, quiet place she had stayed in when she was a hippie. So Mari Lou made the arrangements and we arrived in Hawaii. Well, the accommodation was far from the beach, the little house was livable, but the windows had no covering. Truth be known, it was not very luxurious, so Lew went hunting. Since one of the church's leadership couples was away, the Pastor put us in their lovely house. We now had a car, and we had two great weeks all by ourselves.

We also visited Taiwan and went outside the city to minister at a conference. The accommodation was lovely and modern, but the whole house was made of molded plastic. All the walls were sweating, and everything was wet and cold. I thought I would never be warm and dry again.

On our 50th anniversary we chose to take a cruise from Los Angles to Hawaii and back. We were on a beautiful ship and stopped in seven Hawaiian ports. We enjoyed Hawaii at its best. The ship was our luxurious hotel, with fabulous food, and transportation whenever we wanted it. We explored the ports and towns. They even celebrated us with a luau. It was so special.

We were in Uganda to celebrate RUN Ministries' 20th anniversary and, unknown to us, the leadership of RUN Ministries also chose to celebrate our 50th wedding anniversary while we were there. The Ugandans love a good party, and they know how to put a party on! They had planned a wedding using their traditions, and everything was a complete surprise to us. My dress turned out to be a wedding dress, with a matching African style shirt for Lew. My matron of honor was Deborah Kaweesa, Lew's best man was Pastor Joseph Kibirige, our attendants and ushers were the eldest child of each of our leadership's children, and everyone's attire was African style. Traditionally the brother of the Bride gives her away, so since my brother Hugh was there, he did the honors. Also, in their tradition the groom has to give the brother a large, perfect, live rooster. So Lew came to meet me with a rooster under his arm and, since both men can "ham it up," they discussed what I was worth, and whether Lew was prepared to look after me as well as my family had. Finally they agreed, and Hugh accepted the rooster. By this time the congregation was in gales of laughter.

Then the service started—a full blown wedding! We were asked to say our vows, which we didn't even know about, so we made them up on the spot. Pastor Sam Namatiiti did the ceremony and Pastor Derrill spoke words of counsel regarding the awesomeness of longevity in marriage. One of them had made a beautiful wedding cake, and by tradition the bride has to kneel before the groom and feed him a piece of cake and a drink. Everyone was satisfied that Pastor Marion duly knelt in front of Pastor Lew—amazing. That being done, we were married and ready to start on our second 50 years. They took a "wedding offering" and the congregation, out of their lack, gave us money gifts. We were greatly humbled. They certainly know how to celebrate in great style.

Children

On our wedding day God set in front of me an open invitation to raise up a new generation to follow Him all their ways. Unfortunately, as much as I didn't want to, I made my share of mistakes in raising my daughter. When I look back on the years, I regret those mistakes, but there is nothing I can do about it, so I move forward into the future years.

We experienced our first challenge: a dramatic miscarriage. Our honeymoon baby, a son, and at 16 weeks we lost him. This was enough to scare any man who didn't have any sisters. Lew came home to find me hemorrhaging and near death. The ambulance arrived and rushed me to the hospital. Several blood transfusions later, and with great care, I survived. Lew's composed self and care brought us through that trauma, with our marriage and love stronger and totally intact.

> "Children are a heritage from the Lord,
> The fruit of the womb is a reward.
> Like arrows in the hand of a warrior
> So are the children of one's youth.
> Happy is the man who has his quiver full of them;
> But shall not be ashamed,
> But shall speak with their enemies in the gate."
> —Psalm 127:3–5

I take encouragement from David's mistakes and hope to learn from them. Imagine having your mistakes written in the bestselling book ever written for all the world to read. God never dwells on the negative, and when David repented, God forgave, and it was over. He opened a new door for David to walk through. The ensuing years were not easy, but God brought him through. He became the King and a man after God's heart. God does the same for us. He is faithful.

"I know your works. See, I have set before you an open door,
and no one can shut it; for you have a little strength,
have kept My word, and have not denied My name."
—Revelation 3:8

One of the things David had to contend with was his wayward son Absolam, who had a rebellious heart. His behavior caused David to realize that his mistakes had left scars in his family. Absalom tried to steal the Kingship from David deceitfully, but God had chosen and anointed David King. However, when David was told that Absalom had died in battle, he cried in such deep sorrow, "O my son Absalom, my son, my son Absalom, if only I had died in your place! O Absalom my son, my son!" This caused the entire nation to mourn the death of Absalom, for the King was mourning for his son.

We need to raise up the next generation. Absalom built a monument to himself because he didn't have a son. He tried to build on deceit, claiming titles, fame and loyalties instead of birthing sons. If I don't build sons, I will build a monument. Pass the message on to those who are trustworthy, those that are begotten of the Lamb, my children, and those the Lord gives me as my children.

Years ago Lew and I were challenged to be certain that we took time every summer to do something fun with the family. Sometimes we included meetings on the trip, but we always had a good time, even if somewhat challenging. Usually the trips included whoever was living with us at the time, which with campers and tight quarters make for learning experiences.

In San Francisco we couldn't find a campground, so we parked in a parking lot, and in the morning we found ourselves in a construction site. The girls had to get out of the camper and cross the site to a restaurant washroom, which aroused a response from the workers. Dad had a fit, and we moved on quickly!

On one Sunday in Salt Lake City, we wanted to go to church. We attended a traditional Assembly of God service in the morning, which was just so-so. Dad then looked in the phone book for a more lively church to attend in the evening. He made some phone calls, chose one, called, and got an address and time for their evening service.

Well—when we arrived we discovered it was an African-American church. If you could imagine, one white man and his white wife and three white girls, singing and clapping, enjoying the service amidst of a church full of black folk, it was kind of a spectacle. Talk about alive—my goodness! Lew and I had been in black churches before, but the girls had not, and they were overwhelmed. They found it hard to keep from giggling, and they loved it. In the middle of the song service, we were asked to introduce ourselves and to give a testimony, and so we did.

The Pastor had to leave, and somehow he had twigged onto the fact that Lew was a Pastor. He was so excited that God had provided someone to preach, and then he asked Lew to preach. He did! They ran, they shouted, the organist zipped up and down the keys, and folks were having glory fits. I don't know if there was any outcome, but we had fun. It was amazing.

We met the Hamons in Texas and camped on the beach. We played in the water. Lew and I loved being with Bill and Evelyn, and we caught up on the past years of news. It is so refreshing to have time with longtime friends. The teens swam and enjoyed time together. Since Darlene was a lifeguard we ignored the teens as she watched them, visited some, and enjoyed the sun and water. It is so good to take the family out and about to experience whatever comes along.

At the end of one of our trips to minister in Alberta, Canada we had to rush back to Vancouver to participate in a Family Seminar. We had taken our "girls" with us, since it was summer and we had such a wonderful time together. We were "flying high!"

Traveling at night by road through Jasper, loaded down and squished, the dreaded blue lights began to flash behind us. We were being pulled over by the police! Since Lew was a very disciplined driver, we knew it wasn't for speeding. Whatever could be wrong? Lew rolled down the window, the officer asked for the usual papers, and they were provided, "Where are you going, and where are you coming from?"

"I am a Minister, and I have been preaching in Alberta churches. I'm on my way home to Vancouver," Lew said. The officer looked at me, and then into the back seat where the disheveled girls had awakened and were staring at him. "Who are these women?" he asked.

"My wife and daughters," Lew answered.

He then commanded: "All of you—get out of the car." We did. It was cold, and we were unhappy to say the least.

He made Lew take down the travel box over the trunk and open it, and of course it was full of clothes. He inspected the trunk and the car, and then he put Lew through the paces. He obviously thought Lew was a pimp who had brought his "girls" into Alberta for business. He was looking for drugs. Lew was mortified, and I was furious. The girls were not amused. They just wanted to get back into the warm car.

It wasn't funny at the time, but after he let us go we saw the funny side. Imagine anyone thinking that of Dad—so contrary to the person Dad was. Quite an ending to a wonderful trip!

Grandparents

When we became Grandparents, we were living in Uganda. Because we are Canadians with Landed Immigrant cards in the States, we needed to come back to the USA every two years. When we did, we tried to do something special with the grandsons. When they were babies we helped look after them. As they grew, we took the family somewhere special.

Once we went to Disneyland, another time to Edmonton, then to Florida, traveling down the eastern coast of the USA. We took them to Vancouver, BC and showed them our favorite spots from when we were kids, and where we had lived and worked. We also took them to my nephew's cottage on Main Island, where they went out with him to trap shrimp and crab—a new experience for the boys on the Pacific Ocean.

At one time my father owned a summer cottage on Keats Island, just outside Vancouver, BC. He sold it to a family in the church years ago. My sister and I spent most Augusts there with my Mom. I called the folks who have the cabin now to see if I could rent it for a holiday with my family. She said, "Certainly, let's arrange a date." We did, and with the addition of a friend and his wife and their boat, we spent a week at Keats. It was marvelous, repeating all the rock climbing, swimming and fishing that we used to do.

While at the cottage, we decided to go by boat to visit the youth camp where Lew and I ran youth camps in July every year, which was across the Sechelt Peninsula and up the inlet. What a glorious time it was, as we reminisced and showed the grandsons where we had served the Lord with the youth every summer. Mari Lou wept— it was so special to remember and to have her teen boys there to see and still feel the presence of the Lord in the broken down tabernacle. She had begun the camp experience there as a little girl and grew with it till she was in her teens.

I like to think it is like what Noah did thousands of years ago.

"By faith Noah, being divinely warned of things not yet seen, moved with godly fear, prepared an ark for the saving of his household, by which he condemned the world and became heir of the righteousness which is according to faith."
—Hebrews 11:7

Build an Ark!

A Christian home is a place of safety for families in this wicked and perverse generation. Let's make our homes a "grand central station" where children are always welcome, the cookie jar is always full, and then our kids will be home and happy with their friends, even all through college. Then we won't lose them to the flood of corruption, wickedness and the anti-God attitudes in this generation. It is their music, their fun, and their styles. It is their turn now. As long as they love Jesus it is okay. We can't expect them to be part of what we were, because they are a new generation. As long as we are comfortable with them, they will be comfortable with us.

Jesus warned us:

> "But as the days of Noah were,
> so also will the coming of the Son of Man be.
> For as in the days before the flood
> they were eating and drinking, marrying and giving in
> marriage, until the day that Noah entered the ark,
> and did not know until the flood came and took them all
> away, so also will the coming of the Son of Man be."
> —Matthew 24:37–39

> "My Spirit shall not strive with man forever."
> —Genesis 6:3

> "But Noah found grace in the eyes of the Lord."
> —Genesis 6:8

> "The earth also was corrupt before God,
> and the earth was filled with violence."
> —Genesis 6:11

> "Make yourself an Ark."
> —Genesis 6:14

God sees the condition of man's rebellion against Him and His principles. He is grieved, but God's Grace is upon you. Our world is corrupt, so let's build an ark.

Build an Ark ~ So everyone can see how you have built godliness into your personal life.

Build an Ark ~ A refuge for your spouse, your sons and daughters, your village, your relatives, your friends, for anyone who will listen. Show them again and again the way to be safe is in the Ark.

Build an Ark ~ Give them beauty for the ashes of the world. Preach the gospel, visit the sick, and encourage the broken. Pray! It is hard, continuous work, and invites persecution, but you have the Ark—the only hope for everyone. Invite them in continually.

Build an Ark ~ For anyone who wants to be protected from the everyday life's storms by God's love and grace. The storm will not necessarily go away, but in the midst of it you will be protected and at peace.

Don't ever give up. You possess hope. Stand for righteousness. Don't condemn, but point the way with loving and hopeful persistence.

Just concentrate on being instead of doing. If you are content to be simply yourself, you will become more than yourself. Be instead of doing, then your doing will benefit the Kingdom of God.

I have learned to be creative, not strive, but just be true and honest. I will be glad in God, proud of my faith, appreciate my salvation, celebrate Jesus, and enjoy the best of Him. It is so important for our own children to see Jesus in everything we are and do. **Build an Ark**.

O happy day that fixed my choice
on Thee, my Savior and my God!
Well may this glowing heart rejoice,
and tell its raptures all abroad.

O happy bond that seals my vows
to Him who merits all my love!
Let cheerful anthems fill His house,
while to the sacred shrine I move.

T'is done: the great transaction's done;
I am my Lord's and He is mine;

He drew me and I followed on,
Charmed to confess the voice divine.

Now rest, my long divided heart;
Fixed on this blissful centre rest,
Nor ever from my Lord depart,
with Him of every good possessed.

Happy day, happy day,
when Jesus washed my sins away!
He taught me how to watch and pray,
and live rejoicing every day.

Happy day, happy day,
when Jesus washed my sins away!

—*Philip Doddridge (1755)*

May everything good from God our Father be yours always.

Right: Marion's
Graduation

Below: Dad & Mom
Long Beach

Right: Skipper Lew

Above: Crescent Beach
Camp

Right: The Gang

Above: Lew & Marion at Camp
Below: Engaged

Above: Wedding Day

Below: Names L - R: Britney, Edward,
Mari Lou, Marion, Jeff, Brian, McKenzie

CHAPTER THREE

Pete & RePete

I don't remember when we became Pastor and Sister Pete, but whenever it was, it stuck! In our early years Church was the major part of our lives. We all attended public schools and had friends there, but church was our focus, and all our close friends were there. We had the same faith system and enjoyed the same activities together. Even today those relationships still exist, and when we are together it is like we've never been apart for 40 years.

Mari Lou

On October 6, 1959 the Lord gave us a beautiful little girl. We combined our names and presented her back to Jesus to fulfill her destiny. It has been a love affair between the three of us since day one. She was her Daddy's girl, and never gave us an ounce of trouble except normal growing up adjustments. Early in her life she began to experience the difficulties of being a "PK" (preacher's kid), but that never interfered with her decision to be a true disciple of Jesus Christ.

When we came home from Uganda, as an eight year-old she was so proud of her "mission" and her "show and tell" at school was her artifacts and stories from Uganda. Her teacher insisted she was exaggerating and disciplined her for lying! It was difficult, but she didn't became bitter or angry at her lot in life. She continues to be a true disciple of Jesus. At 16 she made her declaration that her stand for Jesus was hers and not the tag-along experience of her Dad and Mom.

After graduating from Temple Academy in Vancouver, BC, Mari Lou taught in the ACE school in Vancouver and then in Yuba City, California. She attended Yuba College, studying music. Refusing a scholarship with the San Francisco Opera Society, she became our music minister and also taught worship in the Bible School. She spent a year in Belton, South Carolina helping with the music program there. God blessed her with the gifts of administration, teaching and music. She married Jeff Holmes, a wonderful man, and together they gave us two grandchildren, Edward and Brian. Lew and I wrote this Ode to her, with great love and respect for the Woman of God she became as she walked step by step as a true disciple of Jesus Christ.

Ode To Mari Lou
A special miracle
Instantly loved
Brown eyes like Dad
A sweet, easy, contented, cheerful personality.
Mari Lou

"I hit the jackpot"
First Peterson girl
Pastor's Kid
Singing, "I am so Happy" -
a happy, happy, happy musical spirit.
Mari Lou

World traveler
New friends, new language
Boy Cousins

Lovingly and joyfully accepting people of another culture.
Mari Lou

Temple Academy
Sechelt youth camp
Laying on of hands
Developed personal Biblical principles
while building Godly character.
Mari Lou

United States
Yuba College
"Mom, I'm in love."
A true and talented Worshipper,
while a joyful leader and mentor.
Mari Lou

Jeffrey Holmes
Gresham home
New citizenship
The ability to adapt to change with a Godly attitude,
anticipation and gratitude.
Mari Lou

Edward & Brian
Awesome Mom
Public Schools
A personal demonstration of letting your light shine:
"Meet you at the Pole."
Mari Lou

Para Educator
Basketball tournaments
Music Lessons
A loving, patient and compassionate grace for the
unfortunate handicapped teens.
Mari Lou

City Bible Church
Independent Boys
Portland Bible College
A high score in handling the emotional
empty nest syndrome.
Mari Lou

Britney & 'Kenzie
Two Weddings
Family time
The Holmes Clan of six now established
with a very happy Mom.
Mari Lou

Marriage Counselor
Worship Team
Outreach projects
"Leave it for an inheritance for
your children after you forever."
Mari Lou

"Her children respect and bless her;
Her husband joins in with words of praise:
Many women have done wonderful things,
But you've outclassed them all."
Mari Lou Holmes
—Lew & Marion Peterson 2016

Lewis

Life Scripture: "But God forbid that I should boast except in the cross of our Lord Jesus Christ, by whom the world has been crucified to me, and I to the world" (Galatians 6:14).

Lewis was born on February 27, 1937 in Lethbridge, Alberta Canada. He was named Lewis Edward after two of his Mother's brothers. He didn't know much about his extended family. We did make a trip to Norway and met some of them, visiting the farm and seeing where Dad was born. Lew's parents didn't go back to Norway to visit until much later in life, while we were in Uganda. Lew's brother Bob hunted down Dad's family and sent them on a visit. It was a very meaningful trip for Dad after all the years, and the relatives really didn't know where he had gone!

Lew's Norwegian Dad, Nils Olai Pedersen, was born February 5, 1892 in Folgero, Norway. We were privileged to visit Dad's home on the Folgero farm, where Dad's niece is now living. We saw the home where his dad was born, and the chapel with the cemetery for his ancestors all on the property. His Scottish Mother was born August 27, 1912 in Cam'nethan, Scotland. Mom came to Canada with her parents as a child, and Dad crossed the border into Alberta, Canada in his mid-thirties. He found a job on the Allison farm, and at 37 married 16 year-old Sarah Allison. Nils Pedersen, a gentle man, was raised a Lutheran. He came from a family of circuit-riding preachers living among the fjords on Falgro farm. He loved Jesus with all his heart and raised his boys to serve Jesus and be faithful to the house of the Lord. He would sit for hours reading his Norwegian Bible, weeping and telling Lew that the English Bible just didn't tell it like the Norwegian Bible. Lew was like his Dad in personality, but in stature Lew was over 6 feet tall—a big, handsome guy.

In July, 1954 we were at Camp. The presbytery was ministering and Lew was brought up to the front to be ministered to. There was a strong missionary call to China at that time, so it seemed the same call would come to Lew. Suddenly, as David Schoch began to prophecy, he stopped and said, "No." Then he said, "Strange circumstances. From your birth, I called you to pastor in a dark continent, and you will walk among the huts preaching the gospel. You will build churches and disciple my people to walk in my ways... " The presbytery went on for an hour describing Lew's call.

After the service, Lew's Dad came to him weeping and said, "Son we need to talk. Let's walk," and between heart-rending sobs told him the following story:

"In Norway, I was 17 and I had been designated by my family to become the next preacher in the family. It was decided to send me to Cape Town, South Africa for training in the Lutheran Mission there. I did not want to be a preacher, so protesting in my heart, I boarded the ship heading to Cape Town, South Africa. While in the harbor I jumped ship onto an American Ship. When it arrived in New York, I snuck ashore and ran north, ending up in Minnesota (how long he was there he did not say). I finally ran the Canadian border and ended up getting a job on the Allison farm in Alberta, where I met and married your Mother." By this time Lew was speechless, his mind racing, remembering the word from the Lord that morning at camp.

Hesitating, his Dad continued. "There is more. Your birth was traumatic. You were born at home—a large baby in breach position. Your Mother and you were stressed, and it was becoming dangerously life threatening to both of you. The midwife told me that she was afraid she would not be able to save the baby, and probably not your mother either. I thought God was punishing me for running away from ministry, so I went out into the fields and began to call out to God for mercy. "Father please forgive me for running away. Like Jonah, I didn't want to preach! If you will forgive me, please save my wife and the baby, and I will give you this child to fulfill my call to Africa." The Lord obviously answered my prayer. Both your Mother and you lived, and the rest is history." By this time they were both sobbing and thanking the Lord for his great love and grace.

When the excitement cooled down and Lew began to reason in his mind, he was dumfounded. He was 15, and had never been told about his birth. He thought: God knew my passion to be a pastor—but now Africa? Needless to say, this new information set the course for his life, and since he knew my desire to be a missionary to Africa, I was certainly in the picture.

From that day onward, Lew began his study on the Cross of Calvary, discovering the many victories Jesus bought for us on that Cross. He wanted to understand all that Jesus had done for him when He laid down His life for him. What did it entail? How much, how long, would His loving grace end sometime? He had to know. How could Jesus love him so much to trust him with His church—as a Pastor on a mission field? In Africa. Amazing! Him? Lewis Peterson, a bricklayer, a nobody. He wanted to believe it, but just couldn't grasp it. It was his dream, but how could he ever be good enough? He was overwhelmed with the Wonderful grace of God to meet him, call him, and equip him for the work of the ministry. As far as he was concerned he was humbled, scared and joyful all at the same time. At that time he learned the song that became his favorite throughout his life:

The love of God is greater far than tongue
or pen can ever tell,
It goes beyond the highest star and
reaches to the lowest hell.
The guilty pair bowed down with care
God gave His Son to win,
His erring child He reconciled and pardoned from His sin.
Oh love of God, how rich and pure
How measureless and strong.
It shall forever more endure
The saints and angels song.
—Fredrick Leuman (1917)

Nels Peterson & Sons Masonry

His father was an old country stonemason, converted to a brick mason in Canada. Dad Peterson had a great work ethic and trained his boys early in the family business. Lew took an apprenticeship and became a certified Brick Mason. He was a hard worker and it was a strenuous job. They built fireplaces, chimneys, facings on houses, and fireplace facings and repaired boilers in commercial buildings. While he worked brick laying he gradually learned other construction trades. As a result he spent his whole life building wherever he went—Camps, Institutes, Schools, Churches—you name it, he built it!

Vancouver

Lew's family moved to Vancouver, BC when he was five years old. They became members of Glad Tidings Temple, which then was a small Pentecostal mission in the inner city of Vancouver. The Pastor bothered this little boy. He had one glass eye, and when he prayed only one eye closed. He was watching Lew even when he prayed, and that made this boy pray!

He was a typical young man and participated in sports, loved his dogs, enjoyed his friends, and because of living on the Pacific Ocean, loved his boat and all water sports. Also, what guy doesn't have to try a motorcycle? Lew had to. A "Snortin' Norton" was what he called it. Only there was a problem—my Dad wouldn't let me ride with him. So it wasn't long before he discovered this bike thing was not going to work. He finally gave up and shipped it off to Taiwan with a sidecar as transportation for the missionaries. The most important thing in Lew's life was to fulfill the destiny that God had called him to: full time ministry in Africa.

As Lew grew up, my Dad became his pastor. Dad was his hero, and Lew wanted to be just like him. On Saturday evenings Dad would be found at the church, pacing the prayer room, praying loudly and fervently for the services tomorrow. Lew would come to help clean the church, but also to listen to Dad pray. In the winter he shoveled snow off the flat roof of the church, and virtually did anything he could to have a reason to be there in the church. He learned to pray just like Dad. For his entire life Lew was up at 5:00 a.m. to pray and read his Bible, making notes to himself as encouragement for the day. He never doubted that without the undergirding, wonderful grace of Jesus, he would be useless. He needed to possess the power of the Name of Jesus for the day.

After four years in Uganda, East Africa as a missionary pastor to pastors, Lew was instructed to come home from Uganda to be the Assistant Pastor to Dad in our home church in Vancouver, Glad Tidings Temple. This was a surprise and honor, yet it really was not what Lew wanted to do, as he had planned on living his life out in Uganda. However, he learned to accept this decision as the will of God and an opportunity for further training in ministry. As he grew in the Lord he learned that he had to be infused with Jesus. He returned to Uganda for another 13 years, after pastoring 10 years in Canada and 7 years in the USA.

Pastor Peterson

As a Pastor he was kind and caring, a good preacher, strongly prophetic, and a mentor to young men preparing for potential ministry. His calling, together with his personality and his commitment to the church, made him an amazing coach. The up-and-coming young men respected him and enjoyed being with him, and to this day they still speak fondly of his teaching and counsel.

The Glad Tidings congregation loved his fatherly home and hospital visits. He had many adventures, and many "I need you Jesus" moments. In one of his hospital visits to a very ill mother from our congregation, he stopped to chat with her son in the hall, and he was holding his young son in his arms. Suddenly the alarms went off and the father realized that his boy had pulled the fire alarm! Lew went one way and the Dad and son the other, as the fire trucks arrived.

Lew also had his share of night calls. A desperate, anxious lady called one night. Stammering, she finally got her concern out clearly: the power plug had been disconnected days ago. She didn't know it, and now everything in her freezer was thawed, and what was she going to do now? Lew answered her kindly, "Unplug the freezer, and throw the food in the garbage."

Lew led the Tuesday evening believers meeting. One week a man began to share, and his words were "off the wall" so Lew had to sit him down. The man was angry, so after the service he said he was putting a curse on Lew and Lew would be dead within the year. Lew looked at him and said, "Thanks! Now I know I will be alive and well for at least another year." He asked, "How do you know that?" Lew answered, "Because God won't let anything happen to me to prove your foolish predictions!"

The children loved Lew, and he loved them. Children were not allowed on the platform, so they would hang around at the edge of the platform waiting for him to come and give them all a hug. He always talked to the children and knew them all by name. Yes, he was an awesome Pastor and loved God's people. Those were wonderful years, full of adventure and joy. His grace was sufficient for all the trials that came along. He learned and grew.

I wasn't ready to let him go from me, but God had a plan and it was hard, but okay. One day when Lew was retired, Mari Lou and I took him to the specialist. We didn't know what we would find out, but we knew God was in control.

Diagnosed

On June 23, 2010 Dr. Mega said, "Reverend, everything in this MRI of your brain indicates that you should not have been able to continue your life normally. But obviously your faith has kept you this far, so whatever you are doing, keep doing it." I turned from the Doctor's computer, and the images I saw there of Lew's brain put a thousand questions racing through my brain. Then turning to our daughter and me, Dr. Mega said, "This man must not be stressed anymore in any way. Keep him safe." Stressed?

When, Why, Where, How could this happen? We lived a life full of love with adventure, and that lifestyle had become our normal. Lew was God's man. He was amazing, loving, a compassionate servant to the Church, had disciples all over the world, and very seldom complained about anything. He was a peacemaker and a servant—so unselfish. We never thought about stress. We just lived our life as best we could under each circumstance that came along, as we followed what we believed to be God's will for us, and we loved every inch of the journey.

Should I have been aware? We had loved each other since we were 14 and 15 years old and had done everything we could together for over 65 years, so in love with each other, our family and the church. We had only one single desire and that was to serve Jesus, our family and the Church. Just point us in the right direction and we would be there.

I didn't see this coming—or did I? Should I have been more diligent in understanding my man? Looking back, adventure was Lew's life journey. He was always tackling the impossible and loving people, even when the going was tough and no one seemed to understand. He was so compassionate and understanding, and that was the only way I let myself see him.

The same year we were married Lew began his pastoral journey. The decision each time Lew was sent to a new place to pastor, whether it was to Abbotsford, going to or coming from Uganda, wherever, it was without any prior personal discussion with him. It was announced and decided, and he accepted the challenge. He used to tell the stories and laugh about it, but maybe…this could have been a stress point that, knowing him, he would obey and never question. I guess the term used to describe this would be that Lew was a "stuffer." He stuffed his negative feelings deep inside.

We were young and finding our way in every aspect of our life. He had become a husband, a father and a pastor all a 20-month period.

Talk about a crash course! He spent the first 20 years of his ministry in Canada and Uganda. He became a student of the Bible, a walking concordance, a good preacher, and a caring, compassionate pastor. He had a deep prophetic unction as well, strongly emphasized by his booming voice. Lew also earned his BTh Degree through Christian International University. Accomplishing this was something Lew felt he needed to do to make traveling into different countries easier in this day and age, and it made him happy with himself. He had accomplished an educational goal.

After much turmoil in his home church in Canada, we made our own personal decision to move to the United States to travel in ministry for a season and see where the Lord would lead us. The bright light at this point was the marriage of our daughter to Jeffery Holmes, a wonderful American citizen whom we pastored in Yuba City, California. Mari Lou is a wonderful musician, our music minister and a teacher. Lew was so proud of his girl.

We returned to Uganda, living by faith, and began to do our part in restoring Uganda to its former glory. We endured three separate coups, guns and all, with many life-threatening situations, but the Lord brought us through alive and well. During this time Lew experienced the death of his father and his brother. We also had a very serious car wreck that left me hospitalized for a season. I have begun to realize that by the "stressed-out" charts, Lew certainly could have been stressed.

Lew experienced many demonic attempts to "get" him: misunderstandings, verbal attacks, curses, accusations, and false reports. I spent many a night praying over him, and actually saw demons in the room trying to harm him as he slept. I know that demonic power cannot "get" you unless you open the door for them. But I also know they were out there, and they were after my husband.

As the years went by the wear and tear in Lew's body began to show occasionally. Minor but noticeable odd responses and actions would surprise me at moments. Because they were months and sometimes years apart, I didn't comprehend their meaning. We had 13 wonderful years ministering the second time in Uganda, establishing the ministry there that still carries on today, thanks to the resident ministry of my niece and her husband. Our second season in Uganda was certainly the apex of our 50 years of ministry, and Lew still is deeply loved and respected by our Ugandan family.

United States

I was beginning to be aware that Lew was as done as I was, and we needed a break. I knew Lew would never admit it, so I appealed to City Bible Church to bring us home. I needed to get back home where I could get help for our health and future. We moved back to the USA. Lew was diagnosed with Diabetes 2 soon after were home. Yet he was determined not to give in to this disease.

The next year we took a team of young people to Uganda. The team taught our congregation, "I went to the enemy's camp and took back what he stole from me." Lew did exactly that—he took back his health. He carefully watched his diet, obeyed all the rules, and lost over 100 pounds! After trying so many times throughout his life to lose weight, and failing to keep it off, he never regained this weight again. That was the end of his diabetes. The doctors couldn't find it. It was gone completely!

Thinking about the past few years, I pulled out of my memory bank a few unusual happenings that at the time had caught my attention.

- At the Uganda-Kenya border Lew was unusually upset with the border guards, and for him, he behaved erratically.
- During one of our negative moments in Uganda, Lew was unusually vocally defensive concerning his opinion, disrupting a meeting in the process.
- While in Uganda, Lew suffered a heart attack.
- On our first visit to Botswana, as Lew was ministering and introducing us, he said we had one daughter but no grandchildren yet. What? Ed and Brian were both in their

teens already. Lew loved his grandboys, and they loved him. He was alarmed when he realized his mistake.

Uganda

Later on, the RBC Leadership were ready to dedicate RUN Bible Church's new building in Kampala. With a team from Life Center, Centralia, Washington, we went to join in the celebration. Lew found it a difficult time, and I realized that something was not quite right. I watched him experiencing the feeling of extreme rejection. It showed publically, which was not like him. He did not allow himself to think about himself. He really didn't care, yet at this time the feeling affected him very much, and it was obvious. We returned the next year to celebrate RUN Ministries' 20th anniversary. Lew preached on the Sunday Morning and did okay, but I was aware that he wasn't the same.

I realized this would probably be our last trip to Uganda together. I was finally ready to listen to Mari Lou, and when we decided we needed to go for help, Lew's doctor sent him to a social worker, who suggested a slower pace of life and to avoid stress.

A year or so later we were recommended to Dr. Mega at Providence Neurological Specialties PSV MOB, where he diagnosed Lew to have Mild Cognitive Impairment (MCI). At our return visit a year later Dr. Mega confirmed that Lew had Alzheimer's Disease.

Grandson Brian wrote the following about his Gramps: "I remember him walking me through my first sermon outline on a trip to Canada when I was 12 years old. I remember all the jokes he would share with Ed and I, that we could tell were used and reused, but we loved it. We saw him love our Grandmother with everything he had, making her breakfast and bringing her tea in bed every morning."

"I also remember the advice he gave me on our return trip from visiting Africa, while fighting against the Alzheimer's to gather his thoughts. 'Leaders' influence will only go as far as their willingness to lay their lives down for others. Influence becomes a privilege through acts of service, not the appointment of power.'"

Canada

Moving time again, and this time back to the Fraser Valley in British Columbia, Canada. I felt that bringing Lew back to be near his longtime friends would keep him at peace, being in the familiar surroundings of his youth. I believe God gave us almost two more years together, as after 40 years he was again around his Dave buddies. He was later diagnosed with heart disease and vessel degeneration, but because of the Alzheimer's Disease they could not do any repairs to his heart. It would just be too dangerous and would advance the Alzheimer's.

Through it all Lew was so loving, sweet, caring and compassionate. He was mostly silent, listening to my chatter and our music. He loved worship music as well as all the new songs. We sang together along with Spotify radio every morning.

"It is Amazing Grace."

"You make me Brave" declaring: "I am a child of God!"

If he told me once daily, he told me 10 times: "I love you. Thank you for looking after me!" He had his little boy-dog "Ssebo Sir" holding him close, constantly talking to him, with Ssebo Sir literally watching over him.

At the turn of the year we had a trip to the hospital by ambulance, because of the pain in his heart. Through all of this he was fully cognitive, ever loving and kind, always the gentleman, with never a cross word. They treated him and then sent him home to rest. There was really nothing they could do.

February 27, 2017 was Lew's 80th Birthday. He had his second ambulance ride to the hospital, and the family had come to celebrate his birthday. We cancelled his brunch with his "Dave" buddies and celebrated together at the hospital in the lounge, while the doctor kept him in for a few days to have his meds adjusted and for observation. When they sent him home he came with oxygen, and this was a very stressful point for him. He was not happy.

Ten days later, on Tuesday morning, Mike Poulin and Dave McElhoes came to visit, and Lew had phone calls from Pastor Jonathan Biggers and Pastor Marc Estes—such a joy and blessing. Pastor Marc had just returned from Uganda and was so impressed with what he saw there. Lew was so encouraged and seemed relieved. After he hung up the phone, he said to me, "Wow! I guess we did accomplish something!" Mari Lou face-timed him in the evening. They had a good long chat. Soon he was tired, so she said goodbye, and he wanted to go to bed without his oxygen. He fussed and to bed he went. He was restless. He was very distressed with pain from his heart.

Just after midnight on March 8, 2017, Lew sat on the edge of the bed trying to ignore the pain, declaring he would sit for awhile and be okay, and not wanting to go in the ambulance again. Yet I had to call. I didn't know what else to do. He was in such pain, so I finally called. As we waited, I drew him close. I called Mari Lou and kept her on the phone. She talked with her Dad. I could see him failing, and the look in his eyes made me feel that I was losing him. I wanted him to know I was there with him, so I said to him, "do you know who I am?"

I gave him a big kiss, to which he knowingly responded, and the last words he said to me were, "Of course I know who you are...You Are the Love of My Life."

In his unconscious moments I said a tearful goodbye into the ear of the man I had loved beyond life. I know he heard me, as he squeezed my hand acknowledging my words of thanks and love. I will see him again!

I must include here the words from his family:

Mari Lou: "It is an Honor to continue to walk on the path you created, Dad. Thank you for every single stone."

Jeffrey: "Lord, help me to live beyond myself, my own interests, and reach out to other people and give them the same care and love that he gave to me.

Edward: "Grandpa was a man of supreme faith and he believed in God's faithfulness."

Brian: "He was a mentor, a trailblazer, a pastor, a father, a teacher, a missionary, a light in darkness, a rock, a warrior, an intercessor, a jokester, and he was my Grandfather. My Grandfather gave his life for others. He lived a life of service. Now, he gets to see the fruit of his labor. He gets to be free from sickness and finally gets to ask his questions to the Apostle Paul."

Thank you, Jesus, for your redemptive grace, your wonderful love, your righteousness freely given to Lewis Edward Peterson, which he declared around the world. He caught the vision of his destiny, ran the race, and won!

Afterwards

A friend of mine attending a missionary conference was introduced to one of the missionary speakers. He was the founder of Watoto, the Ugandan children's choir and the PAOC Church in Kampala. She asked him, "Do you know the Petersons, they were missionaries in Uganda?" He answered, "Yes." "Do you know that Lewis has passed away?" He paused and commented, "Yes, now there was a Gentle Giant!"

As I write our story, I have rehearsed those last 10 years over and over again, especially those last moments on March 8, 2017. I have recalled what an amazing man of God he was and remembered that when he couldn't recognize and remember names, he would say, "How are you, Man of God?" He was that man!

Thanks to his friends and family, he put his thesis, his thoughts and teachings, together in a book entitled *It's Still the Cross*. We scoured his notes and sermon/seminar tapes and finally published on Amazon in 2010. A quote from Lew's heart:

"Jesus suffered, so we don't have to suffer. Therefore, we accept what Jesus did and we anchor into our lives the purposes of God, and into our destiny wonderful joy. Hallelujah! This doesn't depend on my joy. It depends on His joy. And so when my joy ends, when it has given up and run out, when it is exhausted...I still have joy, because it is His joy."

So wrote my Gentle Giant!

Marion

Both Dad and Mother were born of British parents in the "class" era—Dad in the proper "master/lord" class and Mother in the relaxed "blue-collar" class. Dad was born in Wallington, England in 1904, and Mom in Leeds, England in 1905, and I had the joy of visiting the house where may Mom grew up in Leeds. Mom's family settled in Toronto when she was 15, and Dad arrived in Canada at three years of age. His family settled in Quebec. They were married in 1925 when they were 24 and 23 years of age. They eloped and went on a canoe honeymoon with my Aunt Edith and Uncle Bill!

At a tough time in my teens, I decided I was done with all this discipline stuff and I was going to run away and be happy and free. I told Lew what I wanted to do. Mistake! His advice? "Okay, do what you need to do, but forget me or our dreams. I am going to fulfill God's purpose for my life and this is not part of it!" Obviously I listened. I decided, I like that guy, and continued on the training process together with him.

I was born in Toronto, Ontario, Canada on June 19, 1938. I was named after two of my aunts, my Mother's sister Marion and my Dad's late sister Ethel. Ethel was tragically electrocuted at 16 years old, a very sad and devastating event for the family of boys only! I was honored to be named after her.

When Dad retired and bought a farm on Georgian Bay, we moved to a home in Wiarton, Ontario, so we would be near a school. I met Margaret there in the church, and then in grade one. We became fast friends, and our friendship has continued up to today, 75 years and counting. My parents were believers and raised me to love and serve Jesus. They told me their relationship with Jesus would not work for me, so I had to ask Him into my life for myself.

My pastor was a family friend. I called him Uncle Jack and his wife Aunt Edna. They and their little boy Jess left our church to go to Kenya, East Africa as missionaries. Uncle Jack was my first pastor and I loved them all. I couldn't imagine life without Jess to play with. My heart was broken, and I vowed that one day I would go to Africa and be a missionary also. Of course, I didn't understand the call of God, but as the years passed I realized that it was God placing His call in my heart and His purpose for my life.

Some years later my family travelled across Canada to the west, where I grew up and completed my schooling and training for whatever God had planned for me. As long as it included Africa—and soon, please! I met and married Lew Peterson and we began the journey together. With a passion for preaching the gospel and a desire to build the church, the year we married we began pastoring in a small town in the Fraser Valley. Our daughter Mari Lou was born October 1959—our miracle. Lew's reaction was: "E-e-e-e, I hit the jackpot!" There had been no girls in his family, and he was delighted.

For five long years I begged my Dad to send Lew and me to Africa. I had impatiently waited long enough. My brother Hugh was already there with Audrey and the kids. An amazing revival had spread across Uganda, and I wanted to be there. Word came that Hugh and their son John were sick. We needed to go help! Dad answered my many requests with, "God knows your address and phone number. Just wait for His timing."

Africa

God finally found my address and phone number and called. We were on our way to Uganda at last. It took us such a very long time to get there. We traveled by train across Canada to Halifax, then were at sea for 21 days, till we rounded the cape at Cape Town. Sailing up the coast we stopped in Durban, then Mozambique where the children called Lew "Jumbo." Because Lew was a big man he thought they were being rude, but we found out it was actually "Jambo," which means "Hello" in Swahili. Then we went on to Tanga, Tanzania, where Hugh and Audrey met us.

We enjoyed four amazing years of ministry our first time in Uganda. We later visited my Pastor in Kenya, now in his old age, but still preaching the Gospel. That was a very happy and fulfilling reunion for me.

I had a little knowledge of music, so Hugh asked me to put together a choir. After a year of my playing the accordion while directing the choir, they bought a piano, and that was a great improvement. The choir was a wonderful opportunity for me to express my heart with my love for worship and music. We did musical plays and did a few TV programs. We led worship and provided a great attraction for outreach. My accordion was still a useful tool for the weekly street meetings. We would go out into the countryside, stand under a tree or in the market place, and begin to play and sing. Huge crowds would gather. They seemed to come from nowhere.

I also began a youth club for the teens and young adults. I loved watching them grow in the ways of the Lord. Many of them are still part of the church today, much older but remaining strong disciples of Jesus.

After we had been in Uganda for four years, Dad came to visit and, unknown to us, with the purpose of bringing us back home to Canada to assist him in Glad Tidings, Vancouver. Uganda never left our hearts, and we believed we would one day return to the land of our calling.

Vancouver, BC

"Why would you move from Vancouver? It is the most beautiful area in the world," my friend asked, and then continued, "the Pacific Ocean, the Mountains, and green all year around! The weather is so mild compared to anywhere else in the North. The rain? It is okay—

better than the cold, ice and snow in today's traffic. The mountains are so close, and there you can have all the snow you would desire."

What could I say? My friend was right, but I knew the answer. "Who knows?" you ask. "Jesus." When He calls, you had better answer. We answered, and even though I grew up in Vancouver, I knew I would not always live there, because Africa was calling. We were not looking for a better climate; we were following our wonderful Lord, who knew every step we would take, from the beginning to the end.

Again I found myself involved with whatever my hand found to do. Mari Lou was in school, so I was at the church most days for those hours. Glad Tidings was in transition, Dad was retiring from pastoring, and we were caught in the middle. I remember one such incident. The co-pastor stormed into the printing room, angry as blazes. "Are you wearing lipstick?"

"No."

"What is that on your lips then?"

"Lip salve. "

"Take it off!"

I found out she'd had a call from a mother who had caught her teenager wearing lipstick and blamed me, in order to make it okay. I was a bad example! Talk about confusion. There were lots of misunderstandings and challenges, but God undergirded us with His grace. We learned to pray a lot and trust Him, believing that our being home from Uganda was His will.

I don't remember much of those years. I sang in the choir, led worship, and sometimes I even MC'd the radio broadcast. I didn't ever preach or teach as far as I can remember, except when I had spoken as a youth in a Pioneer Girls service and Wells of Joy. They were busy years, administrating various youth activities such as camps, PNE outreach, winter sports, Youth Ablaze Conference, and the new gym schedules. I also put together the Home Life Group schedule, which I don't think ever clicked very well. We finally moved from the apartment over the noisy gym, purchased our own townhouse in Richmond, and Mari Lou got her drivers license. She and I shared a Volkswagen bug. I think we gave up on ever going back to Uganda. But then, God had a plan!

Yuba City, CA

Ten years went by, Dad had retired, and finally we resigned Glad Tidings and ventured out, not knowing where we were going or what we were going to do. The open door to Uganda was closed by Idi Amin, so that wasn't an option. We settled in Edmonton for a month to look after Peoples Church, while Lawrence and Iris went on vacation. Then we ventured south to Pastor Schoch, where we were scheduled with Dad and Mom for presbytery meetings. We travelled for six months, ministering wherever we were invited, as we grew as a prophetic team. It was amazing.

The phone rang. "Marion, this is Jerry."

"Yes."

" Your Dad has had a heart attack. Can you come right away?" We were in Vancouver to pick up our Green Cards to officially live in the USA. We hurried to Yuba City, and they invited us to stay and pastor the church there. We had met Jerry and the other church leaders already, so we agreed, and there we were, settled in California. Who would have thought? We met a group of wonderful young Jesus people eager to understand the Bible and grow in their spiritual lives.

I administrated an ACE school, organized a Bible College, and began a Pastor's Fellowship. My Dad and Mom had retired in Yuba City, which was an interesting experience for Dad. He insisted that the men had to wear ties on Sunday morning, so he bought them all ties that said in big letters: "Jesus is Lord." Mom and Dad were very loved and respected by those young people, so it was a sad day when Mom passed away while living in Yuba City. Mari Lou met Jeffrey Holmes and they were married in the beautiful new brick building that Lew had built. Then had a lovely outdoor reception in the yard of a 100 year-old heritage home.

Africa, Again

Uganda's borders reopened for tourists. After seven years in Yuba City, while we were visiting in Vancouver, the Glad Tidings leadership asked us if we would like to visit Uganda. Really? I was so excited. "Of course, let's go! Yes!" Our hearts were already open, and we were ready to do more than visit if that was the Lord's plan.

Arriving in Uganda, a devastated country met our eyes and our spirits were shattered. After a couple of weeks we promised to return as quickly as possible to help them. We came home, resigned our church, and within one year we were back again for another season to complete the call that burned continually in our spirits. We were there for 13 years this time. The grace of God was manifested in so many different, miraculous ways, which I will recount in another chapter.

Meanwhile back in the States, our grandsons Edward and Brian were born, and they matured into good husbands and pastors. In Africa we enjoyed wonderful blessings and provision, as well as some disappointing experiences, including facing the guns that come with military coups. Through it all God was with us, and the Lord blessed our labor. A good work was established throughout East Africa, which continues today in ways I never imagined way back when I was just a young girl and didn't understand the call of God on my life.

Portland, Oregon

Lew was not well, and he needed to go back to the West for more complete medical assistance. So after having done my best to fulfill God's appointment for me and to accomplish His call on my life, the time had come to once again head home, this time permanently. With many tears and sad goodbyes to my Ugandan family we returned to our family in the States. We travelled as much as Lew's health would allow, ministering in many countries and encouraging the church wherever we went, telling them about the great harvest of lives in Uganda.

As the years raced by it became obvious that Lew's health was continuing to fail, so I finally took him back home to Canada. I spent 10 years as his caretaker until he passed on to see his Savior. The hardest thing I ever had to do was say a permanent goodbye to Lew. It has taken me a couple of years to allow God's grace to uphold and strengthen me through this grieving process. I wanted to crawl in a hole and never come out. I didn't want to see anyone for any reason. I lost all ambition to do or go anywhere. I felt lost without him.

Then one day, a friend who is a prophet called me and said, "Marion, I feel you need to go for a visit to Uganda to see what the Lord has done since you came back home. You and Lew laid a strong foundation, so go see what has happened." I explained, "We had a dream that we would do that, but the doctor wouldn't let Lew fly."

He reminded me, "Lew is in heaven, Marion. You need to do it. Go!"

I reasoned, "By myself?" I couldn't imagine being in Uganda without Lew. Yet, I did want to be there one more time. "Okay, I will begin to plan the trip." A couple of weeks later, a check arrived in the mail from him to help with finances, and a few months later a second check came from another friend. The trip was totally covered. I didn't have to go alone, as my girlfriend offered to accompany me at her own expense. I knew God was in this plan.

I went, and I returned totally changed. I am not dead! I am still alive! I found the unction was still there—I just had to let it happen, and I felt safe in Uganda. I'm ready for my next season!

As a teen in the 1950's I prayed for Uganda. Then as a wife, mother and pastor in 1964 I arrived in Kampala, and my passion and love has never diminished for the people and churches of Uganda. I am still praying. Uganda is my other home. They are my people. They won my heart in the 60's and I left my heart in Uganda once again over 50 years later, because I love them so much.

Amazing grace! How sweet the sound
That saved a wretch like me.
I once was lost, but now am found;
Was blind, but now I see.
'Twas grace that taught my heart to fear,
And grace my fears relieved.
How precious did that grace appear,
The hour I first believed.
—*John Newton (1779)*

Left: Lew, Mari Lou (2 yrs) & Grandparents

Below: 4 Years

Above: To School

Above Right: Mari Lou and Irene

Right: Graduation

Far Right: Lew and Bob

Left: Jeff & Mari Lou Wedding

Below: Mari Lou Holmes & Her Boys

Right: Mari Lou & Jeff

Above: Mom & Dad Peterson

Right: Mari Lou Holmes & Aunt Ruth

CHAPTER FOUR

Sorry, Please
("Accept my comprehension, please.")

*J*esus told His disciples, "In this manner, therefore, pray." I knew this prayer, which we recited every morning in school. I was a disciple of Jesus and I knew what it meant and why it said what it said, but at that point I didn't realize the impact it would have on my life.

I'm Sorry, Forgive Me Please

Sometime in my teens, I heard a speaker say (referring to Jesus' words) that if we don't forgive those who offend us, then He won't forgive us of our offences to others and—I assumed—to Him. I sat up and took notice. With a personality like mine, I knew I already must have offended someone along the way—probably many. After digesting that statement I purposed to be careful. I would be quick to ask forgiveness from others and from the Lord. The other side of the coin was, would I be willing to forgive whoever offended me? For me, that seemed it would be more difficult.

The first step is to say, "I'm Sorry." As the years went by I found this principle wasn't always easy. Either people didn't know I had been offended, or I didn't know I had offended someone. Then when I would speak to them they would now be offended, or I would be offended. So I had to learn how to approach the situation and how

I should react. It was a learning curve, but I was determined, and I have worked on it my whole life.

I discovered that saying sorry too much is irritating to some, because it became irritating to me. "There is nothing for you to be sorry about," was often the response. I felt I needed to be sorry, but they didn't. So I found other ways to say it, like, "That must be difficult for you," or, "My goodness," or, "I feel your pain," or sometimes, "Let me pray for you."

Living in Uganda didn't help my problem because they say in English a literal translation from their language that means, "Is it okay for me to be sorry for this?" or, "Is it my business to be sorry, because I want you to know my compassion, but I want your permission." "Sorry please." Now you reply, "It is fine, and thank you for caring or understanding or listening to me," whichever is appropriate.

The second step is to acknowledge forgiveness by saying, "I forgive you," or, "Will you forgive me?" This is another situation that is hard for human nature to understand. We are to forgive no matter what, because He has set the example by forgiving us always when we ask for it—nothing held back. Jesus has provided forgiveness for us in every aspect of our lives and readily forgives us even when we don't appreciate it. When we think of His provision, we think of menial things like food, money, housing, job, etc., but His provision includes much more than that. It is a heart condition, no matter who or what we forgive. Sometimes trust is in question, but forgiveness is tied to eternity and we must never withold it.

Over 50 years ago I began to coach a woman who had ignored a principle that Jesus had placed in her life very early in her childhood through Godly parents. She was a pastor's wife with a very strong and accepted ministry and her husband loved her deeply. There was no abuse, and he was totally embraced by the ministry, as she was. It was their life's dream together, and they loved the church and everyone they served.

When I asked her why, there was no reason!

She was deceived by a good friend of her husband's family, a handsome man who used flattery, endless money, and a careless attitude toward the ways of the world. He was very successful financially. After several months of ignoring the prodding of the Holy Spirit by stepping over the line with him, she finally realized she had been parking her life on the correct side of the line, while hopping, climbing, and crawling over it to enjoy the "pleasure of sin for a season." What a fool she was to risk her life, her children, their ministry, the church her extended family. She made the right decision, cut it off immediately, and came for help.

Together we met with the pastor and her. He forgave her with all the love he had for her, and then she and her husband met together with the man. She took all the blame, asked for his forgiveness, and gave back all the gifts that he had given her. Her husband also forgave him.

Together she and her husband cut off the relationship, with no visits or conversations. The line was drawn clearly again, and together they began a new journey that turned out to be the best years of their ministry. She asked the Lord to make her hate the sin, just like God hates sin (not the person), but she needed to run away in the other direction.

The incident did not become public knowledge. Only Jesus, the couple, myself, and the pastor knew. She "came to herself" like the Prodigal who came home to his father, and like King David. When the enemy had stolen everything from him, and even his men had turned against him, he encouraged himself in the Lord and pursued and recovered all. Since she had been forgiven by all those who knew—Jesus, her husband, the pastor and me—she was free to carry on in the call of God for their lives. Her Redeemer had covered her sin by His blood. Thank you, Jesus.

"If only" has been her hardest battle, forgiving herself. She can't believe she allowed something like that to happen to her. The enemy, the condemner, still wants to destroy her, but Jesus, the forgiver, reminds her to hang onto Him in those times when she has to deal with her memory-computer. Doubts spring up, and it all seems like a bad dream. Many years have passed, and today her faith and confidence are strong. They have continued to minister and are being used of God in marvelous ways.

"My brethren, count it all joy when you fall into trials,
knowing that the testing of your faith produces patience.
But let patience have its perfect work,
that you may be perfect and complete lacking nothing."
—James 1:2–4

Offences

Keep short accounts. If you need forgiveness, go ask for it. If you need to forgive, do it quickly and without fear, because God commands us do so. My pastor called me. "Marion, (naming the person) said she had a problem with you, that you were not easy to get along with, and that she couldn't continue to work with you." This upset me. I know I am strongly opinionated. I am often wrong in my approach to people, and can come across as a "know-it-all." I told the pastor I was sorry. Then I called her and apologized and asked her to forgive me. The next day the pastor said to me, "You amaze me. How can you do that so easily?" It was then that I understood the work the Holy Spirit had been doing in me down through the years, molding me and teaching me to live and conduct my life by His principles.

Jesus warned us that offences would come as long as the world and humans were upon it. Being offended is part of being a leader, and yes, even in the church. Dad used to say, "You can't please all of the people all the time, but it would be nice if you could part of the time." Now, after all these years of ministry, I have to agree with him. As a preacher's kid I could do little right and became the example to the congregation. Dad would call me out publically in order to correct some other teen who was misbehaving. Did it hurt my feelings? Yes. Could I do anything about it? No.

Standing in the foyer of the church after the morning service with my friends, I was laughing and carrying on with them as young girls can do. I said something that met with the disapproval of a leader standing by, and she slapped me across the face! Was I offended? Yes. Could I do anything about it? No.

I was told by a respected mother that I was favored by my father, and that was why I was a Pioneer Girl leader and a Sunday School teacher; why I played the accordion at the street meetings, and played piano; why I taught at the mission, and that all pastors' children were favored, leaving the other girls out. Was I hurt? Yes. Could I do anything about it? No.

My father refused for me to have my girlfriends as bridesmaids in my wedding because that would show favoritism. Was I offended? Yes. Could I do anything about it? No.

"Woe to the world because of offences.
For offences must come but woe to that man
by whom the offense comes!"
—Matthew 18:7

Jesus was allowing me to be worked over but I didn't like it! As I matured I came to understand that it was for His purpose, and that I needed to learn to walk in His ways to become all He desired me to be. Put all that together, with all the experiences that followed, and by His grace, mercy and love I felt Him undergird me, even when I didn't understand what was going on.

Thank You

In looking for photos I found this birthday letter that Lew received from one of the couples we loved and nurtured threw the years. Lew had dedicated their daughter. Pasted onto the letter are pictures of them as young folk, and one of Lew with their baby girl. Today, many years later, we don't live in the same country, and they are grandparents. Lew is gone, and they still look after me in a long distance way. Here is what they said so long ago:

"Bro Pete, Phil 1:5. Every time I think of you I thank my God. You have touched our lives for so many years. You have blessed us with the love of God that flowed through you. Our early days at Glad Tidings are full of wonderful memories, Sunday School, boys and girls clubs, youth group, skating, camp. We saw your faithfulness and commitment, and something was planted in our lives.

We took some of our first ministry steps with you and Sis Pete in Wells of Joy and working together in the gym at Youth Ablaze. We remember heading toward your office one day and seeing you both on your knees. You were interceding for the young people—us included. You encouraged and nurtured the gifts of God in our lives.

It was such a boost to us that people we respected so much had confidence in us. We had fun with you, and now we so enjoy your friendship. You have blessed our children, although they never got to meet Betsy Ann! Thank you for investing your life into ours. HAPPY BIRTHDAY!"

Forgiveness

Later in our journey we were at a conference in Kentucky with the Hamons, and the speaker was talking about the Father's love. He had been a professional fisherman and talked about having to make it over the bar with his boat, to get out beyond to the smooth water to get the best catch. He described the danger, and how getting to the peaceful waters took great skill. You had to do it at the right time. He enlarged on the fact of the timing of the Lord, on occasions when He wanted to dig deep into our lives to dig out something that was not pleasing to him—something in our lives that needed to be taken care of. It might be a need to forgive someone, especially if your natural father hinders your ability to receive the love of our Heavenly Father.

I had never thought about it, but his words zeroed in on me. I suddenly realized I had buried a problem and had pushed it so deep that I didn't even know it was there—the resentment against my

Dad for his treatment of me as a teen and a young woman. I needed to forgive my Dad. I hit the altar, on my face, sobbing, forgiving my Father. It was quite a storm and a deep, rough bar to cross. Lew, Bill and Evelyn helped me safely over it, and that deep resentment was washed away as I climbed onto the lap of my Heavenly Father and let Him hold me, as I accepted His love in a brand new way.

This is how it works:

> "If we die with him, we'll live with him,
> If we stick it out with him, we'll rule with him,
> If we turn our backs on him, he'll turn his back on us,
> If we give up on him, he does not give up—for
> there's no way he can be false to himself."
> —2 Timothy 2:11–13 MSG

Because of the burdens of life and the changes of seasons, our Joy and our Song become challenged. Sometimes we even become irritated and hard to get along with. We don't want to, but things are different, and we don't like change. Seasons of life come and go, and I have had to adjust to them—some not so bad, and others very difficult—some I have been thankful for, and others not so much.

My seasons in Uganda, East Africa were a joy, yet with tears. The childhood and teen seasons were sometimes a struggle; my seasons of ministry were growing, maturing seasons; travel was sometimes good and sometimes not so good. So far I have made it through to this season of my life, which has been the hardest without Lewis, but He has brought me through with a high hand.

Thinking about the changes of my life seasons reminds me of the unchanging God I serve. How thankful I am that with all the change around me He never changes. He abides faithfully. The seasons of my life change, but my faith has an anchor and remains steadfast.

Build Yourself Up

Jude concludes with a wonderful encouragement and admonition for the child of God during their seasons of change. "Building ourselves on your most holy faith." Yes, it is a new season. There are challenges. Things are different and perhaps difficult. We must build ourselves up, encourage ourselves, and be an instrument of encouragement to others. Jude tells us how: " . . . praying in the Holy Spirit." Thank God for the death, burial and resurrection of Jesus, for His ascension and His promise to send the Holy Spirit to be our comforter. As we pray in His power we are built up in our faith.

During my life seasons of change, I hung on to the admonition of Jude seriously, by building myself up, praying in the Holy Spirit and believing God for holy results.

> Keep yourself in God's love,
> Experience His mercy,
> Enjoy the provision of eternal life,
> Reach out with compassion,
> Be a diligent witness,
> Put your full trust in Him,
> Accept His provision,
> Live in His presence
> With exceeding JOY!
> —see Jude 20–25

We were in the frozen north of Canada, and one of the Inuk church leaders, going out with the skidoo over the tundra, asked us if we wanted to go for a ride. It would have to be on the heavy, rough sleigh, because Laura Lynn was going to ride on the back of the skidoo behind him. "Yes," we said enthusiastically, and off we went, all bundled up against the cold. It was a thrill to be whizzing along on the frozen ice—miles and miles of white, and so cold.

Suddenly we went over a little hump and Laura Lynn flipped off the skidoo. Lew rolled off the sleigh as it rolled over her. Lew yelled as he ran back to her. Lew's weight off the sled caused the driver to look over his shoulder, and as he circled back we were already loudly praying in the Holy Spirit. Jesus came down, and her injuries were only a broken arm! They flew her out to the hospital to have her checked, and by her life today we know, and are so thankful, that

God had a plan for Laura Lynn, and it was not thwarted that day. Looking at that scar today, we rejoice in His protection.

We knew better, because it was too late and too dark for us to be driving friends back to their residence. Suddenly, there stood an army soldier in front of the car, telling us to stop. Armed with an AK-47, he approached Lew on the driver's side. At the same time, from the back seat Joyce yelled at me, "Roll up your window!" Furiously rolling up the window, I saw a soldier with a knife in his hand coming toward me. As the point scraped the window I said, "Pray in the

Spirit as loud as you can!" to Joyce and Cecil.

Meanwhile, the soldier was commanding Lew to get out of the car. We began to yell, praying in the Spirit. The Soldier at Lew's window again told him, "Get out of the car."

My faith was building, and I said to Lew, "Tell him: 'In the name of Jesus, put down that gun.'" He did just that, while hiding the keys under his leg so the soldier couldn't reach in and grab them. Our friends and I began yelling and praying in the Spirit.

The soldier commanded him again. "Get out of the car." By this time the other soldiers had come around and were just standing there.

We were yelling in the Spirit, and Lew said, "I am going now to take my friends home. Excuse me, please." Lew stepped on the gas and we got out of there, praying that he wouldn't shoot. Thank you, Lord, for your protection, and for the power of the Holy Spirit in that car.

> "Therefore do not cast away your confidence
> which has great reward.
> For you have need of endurance
> so that after you have done the will of God,
> you may receive the promise . . .
> for the just shall live by faith!"
> —Hebrews 10:35–38

I become overwhelmed with thanksgiving to My Lord for
allowing us to be used by Him in building His Kingdom.

Stand up, stand up for Jesus! Ye soldiers of the cross;
Lift high His royal banner, It must not suffer loss.
From vict'ry unto vict'ry, His army shall He lead,
Till every foe is vanquished, And Christ is Lord indeed.

Forth to the mighty conflict, In this, His glorious day,
Ye that are men now serve Him
Against unnumbered foes;
Let courage rise with danger,
And strength to strength oppose.
—G. Duffield (1858)

After we had returned permanently from Uganda, we received the following email. I am printing it just as we received it, so you can enjoy it also.

Dear Mum & Dad,

I just want to thank you both for obeying God's voice to come to Uganda and plant Godly seeds in us. When you talk about a renewed Passion for Missions, I know exactly what you mean. That is exactly who you were and still are even today. WOOOO!!! Your blood is MISSIONS. I pray that that same zeal and passion will be upon your sons and daughters you raised. Looking forward to being with you in the Conference, I love you and am always very thankful for all you invested in us. Rejoice, there is a strong trail behind you. Your Mission time was properly used with good fruit, and Winnie and I, as well as many others I know here agree.

—Joseph

Hi, Dad and Mum,

Thanks for the labor you put in the work of Christ. I am a fruit of your labor. You did not labor in vain. I pray that the good Lord will reward and refresh you.

— Anna

I always remember you as my dear parents. Thank you for the love and your very lives you poured out for us and on us. Peter and I are what we are because of your coming to Uganda. May the Lord bless you abundantly.

— Harriet Magambo

I want you, Dad and Mum, to know that I have precious memories of you. The way you raised and inspired so many of us to love and serve Christ. I remember before you left in 1997, you Pastor Marion, specifically told me that you wanted to find me teaching in the Institute the next time you came back. Since then I have always taught. The ministry is growing from Glory to Glory because of the foundation you laid. I will always be grateful and God will reward you.

—Francis

Pastors Marion and Peterson: Thank you for loving me. May the Lord bless you and give you more years as He did to Hezekiah. Greet my Mari Lou and family – I love you all.

—Grandma Flo

Praise be to God dear Pastors. First of all I want to give thanks to the Lord God almighty for sending you to us. We are all doing well. We have three sons now. From my childhood (Boaz) you raised me and as a teen showed Faith the way to Jesus – we will never forget. We wish you a great time of love during this season and our prayer is that God will richly bless and prosper you as you continue with the Great Commission that is our heritage and destiny.

— Boaz and Faith

All hail the pow'r of Jesus' Name! Let angels prostrate fall;
Bring forth the royal diadem,
And crown Him Lord of all!

Ye chosen seed of Israel's race, Ye ransomed from the fall,|
Hail Him Who saves you by His grace,
And crown Him Lord of all!

Let every kindred, every tribe On this terrestrial ball
To Him all majesty ascribe,
And crown Him Lord of all!
—E. Perronet (1790)

Favor

One of the hardest things for me to grasp was to accept that no matter what I did wrong, He still loved and favored me whether in blessings, disappointments, or challenges—the good, the bad and the ugly. His love wasn't conditional to my behavior. When Job was going through his trials, he made an interesting statement:

> "You have granted me life and favor
> and your care has preserved my spirit."
> —Job 10:12

He cares, no matter what I do, and He does not remove His favor. His favor gives me purpose and helps me make my goals to be His goals for me. When everything goes wrong, His favor hovers over me to do me good. With Redemption comes His favor. It never goes away.

> "For whoever finds me, finds life
> and obtains favor from the Lord."
> —Proverbs 8:35

> "His anger is but for a moment,
> weeping may endure for a night
> but His favor is for life."
> —Psalm 30:5

Our problem is that we think we know ourselves, yet He knows what will happen to us far better than we do. You see, He loves us.

Every time I go into a crowded parking lot I ask Him for a space to be available for me. I don't know how He arranges it, but sure enough He does, over and over again. He knows how painful it is for me to walk, so he favors me!

In Uganda we were having some problems with our resident permit, and we couldn't understand why. We wondered if there was a problem with some person or church complaining about something we had done, but nevertheless the file could not be found. During our last time in the States there had been a prophetic word that warned us trouble was coming, and our God would take care of it. Now here was the trouble—what to do? Then, when we were back again in Canada we were still concerned, and there came a word again. This time the prophet said, "You are having trouble with a permit. They are telling you that your file must be lost. Go back and tell them it is beside the wall and the file cabinet, and I will give you favor."

Upon returning to Uganda, Lew went to the immigration office once more. They told him yet again, "Your file is still lost, you need to apply again." Lew pointed to the file cabinet by the wall and said, "It is right there, between the cabinet and the wall—please look."

There it was! We received our permits that day with no problem! We were so thankful for the favor of the Lord.

We had come home from Uganda to live permanently. Money was tight, so I decided to look for a job. Someone suggested I look for a job with the State of Oregon, so the hunt began. I applied for one as an Administrative Assistant in a new Tri-County BCD office (Building Codes Division). Now I knew that was a long shot, since I only had various buckets of experience from our church offices, the ACE school, the Institute in Uganda, and a BA in Theology. Anyway, I went for the interview, and they hired me! Everyone was shocked—including me. After I had been there a year, they asked me to be on the hiring committee. That really amazed me. I finally asked the office manager, "Why did you hire me? I'm over 60 years old and had no business experience. She said, "We liked your spirit. There was something different about you." Thank you, Jesus, for your favor!

I am thinking of Queen Esther, a captive who did not originate from the provinces of King Ahasuerus. Esther was raised by her uncle, and as captives they lived in one of the King's provinces. Because Esther was among the most beautiful young virgins in the land, she was chosen, among others, to be considered in the search for a new Queen. In order to be prepared, Esther, along with all the other virgins, moved into Shushan Palace. She was apprehensive, because technically she was a captive in a foreign land. However, she submitted herself to the advice of her Uncle Mordecai, who worked as a guard, and Hegai, the custodian of these young women.

After all was said and done, The King chose Esther to be his new Queen.

"Now the King loved Esther more than all the other women,
and she obtained grace and favor in his sight
more than all the virgins;
so he set the royal crown upon her head

and made her queen instead of Vashti."
—Esther 2:17

I am favored of the King of Kings! I am His Queen! He loves me! One of the king's princes knew that Esther was a captive, and a Jew, and manipulated the King to decree that all the captive Jews in all the land must be killed. When Uncle Mordecai heard the decree, he went to Esther as Queen, asking her to plea for the lives of the captives. Did she think that she, a Jew, would escape? The decree applied to her as much as to the other Jews. Esther replied:

"Go, gather all the Jews who are present in
Shushan and fast for me;
neither eat or drink for three days, night or day.
My maids and I will fast likewise.
And so I will go to the king, which is against the law;
and if I perish, I perish!"
—Esther 4:16

Can you imagine how scared Esther was? She prepared herself and stood in the court. She was as good as dead. What if he became angry? What if he ordered her killed on the spot? Or would he hold out his scepter, the symbol of his authority, indicating she was accepted to be in the court?

"So it was, when the king saw Queen Esther
standing in the court,
that she found favor in his sight,
and the king held out to Esther the golden scepter
that was in his hand.
Then Esther went near and touched the top of the scepter."
—Esther 5:2

All she had to do was touch the top of the scepter to accept his approval, his favor, and his authority. All I have to do is enter into his God's presence with thanksgiving and praise, and His authority, His favor is mine. Just touch His scepter. He has given me his authority. His scepter is stretched out to me, because He has promised it to me. I am righteous. He is My Lord, and I am His disciple. No sinful authority can destroy me.

"For the scepter of wickedness shall not rest
on the land allotted to the righteous."
—Psalm 125:3

"Your throne, O God is forever and ever;
A scepter of righteousness is the scepter of your kingdom.
You love righteousness and hate wickedness."
—Psalm 45:6

You and I have God's favor forever. Like Esther, we have the opportunity to save the next generation. Think about it. As different as this new generation is, we have a common ancestor. This is what a generation is—a succession of a common ancestor.

If I perish, I perish. Touch that scepter, accept His favor, and plead for the next generation to live. The answer was to fight for your life! The king couldn't change his decree, but he could make a new decree, that the Jews *could fight for their lives.*

Our message to the next generation is: Touch His presence and fight for your life. We must not criticize, but accept and encourage every generation alive. I have the King's favor, so what I must do is rise up in His righteous authority that He has given to me.

- I am favored of the King of Kings.
- I have his righteous authority.
- I will touch His presence.
- I will reach my world.

I am ready for the greatest display of God to the world today. I have a job to do to see His display of righteousness, so I must go into my world and demonstrate His favor.

"Ask of me, and I will give you the nations
for your inheritance
and the ends of the earth for your possession."
—Psalm 2:8

His favor given to us includes His roles as our provider, councilor, advisor, instructor, consultant, burden bearer, and supplier of all the day-to-day amenities that life requires. Because of the nature of time, there is only one direction to travel and that is forward. Interestingly, since conception we move forward. Our eyes, hands and feet all face forward. Even when we want to go backwards, still they face forward. God's plan in creating humanity is that man would continually move ahead through the generations of time, ever moving to fulfill his destiny in the will of God.

Generations

As one generation follows another we are moving forward. Think of it: *You are the ancestor of someone yet to come!* No wonder God is more interested in generations than in congregations. Congregations become stuck and stale in their style, methods, programs, music and standards, while God wants his redeemed children to keep moving ahead. The Apostle Paul expressed his determination. "I've got my eye on the goal, where God is beckoning us onward—to Jesus. I'm off and running, and I'm not turning back."

One of the challenges of the human body in old age is to move! The joints ache, weariness sets in, and the mind slows as the years go by. It is too easy to look back to the "good ol' days." Yesterday becomes a fantasy in our memory. Yes, they were good days. They were exactly that: good old days, long gone and now behind us. Let us live *for* today and in today! The first steps have been made, and the climb continues, going up one stage after another with every generation. In 1517 Martin Luther began the climb, when his Ninety-five Theses kickstarted the Reformation in Germany. We don't want to get stuck on a plateau, while this generation continues the climb to the top. We must join them!

There is a "now" generation. They don't need us to remind them of our generation's methods, or what we did. They need us to help them understand how to move forward from where we progressed in our generation. Was my generation God's favorite? Of course not. A wise pastor in our past constantly reminded his congregation: "God meets every generation in their day." God is meeting this generation!

In coming home from Africa we expected to be challenged by many changes, so we made the decision to "go with the flow" and move ahead with the new generation both in home, business, city and church life. Yes, the momentum was rapid, and at times extremely challenging, but we realized that different isn't wrong, it is just different. We still press forward toward the prize, being who we are at this season, doing our best to secure this generation by loving them and serving Jesus, establishing the Kingdom of God in the earth. Challenging, isn't it? Let's accept the challenge, and move forward with this generation, as it is the only way to be part of the completed job.

I'm pressing on the upward way, new heights
I'm gaining every day
Still praying as I'm onward bound,
Lord, plant my feet on higher ground.
Lord lift me up and let me stand By faith
on heaven's table land.
A higher plane than I have found,
Lord, plant my feet on higher ground.
—Johnson Oatman, Jr. / Chas H. Gabriel

Roads and Vehicles

When it comes to cars and roads, we have seen the favor and grace of God in so many ways. We have felt His provision and His banner over us in His love and protection. When we first arrived in Uganda, the potholes in the main roads were huge craters left from the bombs. If small cars were going too slow, they would get stuck in them. Most of the side roads are still dirt and not graded, and the bumps and ruts make for a very rough ride.

When Shirley and I were visiting recently, Pastor Joseph was taking us home when the front of the car went into a deep rut by the side of the road. He managed to back out and park the car, then we walked up hill in the mud for the next half mile or more to Dr. Irene's house. For the young folks that would not be so bad, but for us grandmas it was quite an undertaking. Joseph was so kind, walking us up one at a time so we wouldn't slide and fall. Yes, I love Uganda!

Roadblocks

There were so many roadblocks on the roads during and after the war in those days. Drivers learned to be polite and the passengers learned to pray in the Spirit! One of the young boys who was living with us walked everywhere, and at one roadblock he was accused of stealing the rubber boots he was wearing—that we had bought for him—and they took him to jail. In the jail Phillip spent every day preaching the gospel at the top of his voice and praying in the Spirit out loud!

We were worried about what had happened to him. We didn't need to worry, because he was enjoying himself in jail. Finally the guards couldn't take it any more, so they let him go. Without his boots, of course. He turned up at home in his stocking feet, but so happy that he could witness and by that be set free. He felt like the Apostle Paul, and he made the earth quake with his voice! His one desire was to be a "Voice for Jesus."

We experienced our share of those roadblocks. Once when we were returning from meetings in Musaka, a government coup had started and we drove furiously, hurrying to the safety of our home in Kampala. We rounded a curve and there was a roadblock! We were passing on a wet, swampy side road, and there they were, all three of them with their AK-47s, looking very angry and official. Lew rolled his window down a crack and Shari and I looked straight ahead, holding our breath and praying fervently.

The soldier asked us where we were going. Lew said "Home—just over there," pointing to the hill on the left. Pointing at me, they said, "Who is that?" "My wife, and a friend," Lew replied. He took his time looking around and finally let us drive on. What a relief. His presence was with us. Thank you, Jesus.

Another time Lew and I were traveling alone (not wise) to hold a regional meeting for MFI-EA, and we came across a roadblock. The soldiers were young, very threatening, and obviously proud of their authority. We stopped, and they motioned Lew out of the car. One soldier began to punch Lew like he was boxing.

He commanded, "Passports!" I had them ready and handed them to Lew. He looked at them upside down, then he looked at me in the car and said, "Who is that?"

"My wife," Lew answered.

"Oh," he said. "I have always wanted a Canadian wife," and began to try to get Lew to box with him.

I was praying in the Spirit, trying not to panic. Lew just stood there, not moving a muscle. The soldier tried so hard to get Lew to hit him. Thank God for His favor upon us, and Lew's calm nature. The soldier gave up and motioned us to go. We moved away quickly, praying that he wouldn't shoot. Jesus, you are so good. Thank you for your protection and peace.

One more story. We were headed to Kenya to shop and minster with Jim and Barbara Webb. Just before the border there was always a roadblock. We were expecting it, so we were not surprised when they motioned us to stop. They wanted all of us to get out. Thankfully, we were not alone, and we had Joseph with us. "Passports" they commanded. "Where are you going?" they asked. "To Niarobi."

"What for?"

"To visit friends and shop," Lew replied.

"For what?"

"Groceries."

On and on they went, just to show their authority, which we knew they didn't have, but there was nothing we could do but answer and pray. I don't think they could have stopped us from going on, but it certainly was nerve-racking.

Other than roadblocks, another road thing that happens in Uganda is when officials travel. They travel with escorts. The length of the "parade" depends on the importance of the person, or their destination. After a war, most of them are soldiers with their AK-47s, ready to shoot anyone in their way, and they are threatening. We have had many a close call, by not being out of their way quickly enough or far enough away.

Vehicles

Uganda roads are hard on vehicles. We began with a 4W Drive Nissan pickup, then a Passat sedan, which we sold to help by the Institute property. After that we purchased rebuilt army jeeps and a Van to transport folk from the Institute property to Kampala to church meetings. Our road into the property was horrendous. Dirt, loose gravel, rocks, potholes—just terrible, and it wore the vehicles out too quickly. The district might grade it once a year!

Stealing vehicles was always a big threat. In one coup we had our new Nissan 4W-drive pickup stolen and hidden in the forest on one of the Kampala hills. A believer saw it and came running to tell the pastor he had seen it and where. When we went to get it, it was out of gas, two tires had been shot out, and the router was gone! We were sure that the soldiers had done the damage on purpose so no one else would steal this new vehicle, and they planned to come back for it.

While I stood guarding the vehicle with a policeman, Lew went with the pastor to get tires and gas. Having accomplished that, he returned to put on the tires and pour in the gas. We pushed the pickup downhill, through the main street downtown, and up our hill to the house (about three miles), put it in the garage, locked it in, and hid the keys.

Car problems are not something I know anything about, and that was the scariest that I ever want to experience again. Lew taught me to drive when I was 17. My dad wouldn't let me drive his car, and when Lew offered to teach me I asked Dad if it was okay. He said, "If Lew's dumb enough to let you ruin his car, that is up to him." So Lew was dumb enough, and I have a pretty good 63-year driving record. Now when it comes to a lead foot that is a different story. I do everything fast, including driving!

Here is my driving record: I have only three bumps in my years of driving, and two of them were when backing up. My first bump was early in my driving experience. At Capilano Canyon I saw a space in the parking lot and zip—I put it in reverse—and bang, I hit car behind. Forgot to use my mirrors. My second bump was learning to drive an automatic Buick. I had stopped at a sign, and when I took my foot off the brake the car kept going forward! My third bump experience was about five years ago in the underground parking garage of a condo. I backed into a cement post with our new car. I wasn't very popular!

Homes

Moving my home has been a regular occurrence in my life. In fact, when you average it out, I moved every 21/2 years in my lifetime, sometimes several times in the same city. Then I moved again last year. I can't say every move was an upgrade, but if it wasn't we renovated and made it like new, and then moved again. We joked about renting in Uganda. Our mission was called RUN, "Restore Uganda Now" one house at a time. We would just get the house fixed up nicely, and feel happy with it, and then the owner would double the rent, because now it was lovely, with no more appearance of war.

I am thankful that My Lord favors me, loves me, and is my protecting banner. He is my provider for everything I need, and I am ready to forgive and forget as I move on in my new season of life.

Standing on the promises of Christ my King,
Thro' eternal ages let His praises ring;
Glory in the highest, I will shout and sing,
Standing on the promises of God.

Standing on the promises of Christ the Lord,
Bound to Him eternally by love's strong cord,
Overcoming daily with the Spirit's sword,
Standing on the promises of God.

Standing, standing, Standing on the promises
of God my Savior.
Standing, standing, I'm standing on the promises of God.
—R. Kelso Carter (1886)

What Do I See?

My question is, "What do I see?" Elijah saw something his servant couldn't see. He heard a sound his servant couldn't hear. At the word of Elijah, in judgment from God for Ahab's idolatry there came famine in the land. The circumstances were very real. The widow woman with her son was ready to give up and die. The prophets of Baal were desperate to end the famine. Ahab would not admit his sin and set out to prove his idolatry, but Elijah proves to all that, "The Lord, He is God!"

Elijah declared to Ahab what he heard: "There is a sound of abundance of rain!"

He sent his servant to look toward the sea. "What do you see?"

"Nothing!"

"Look again."

He said seven times, "Nothing!"

Then . . . "there is a cloud the size of a man's hand.

"Elijah said, "Run! Tell Ahab to get a move on before he gets his chariot stuck in the mud! "For there is the sound of an abundance of rain" (1 Kings 18:41).

What do you see? What do you hear? God is in control. He has already sent the answer to your famine. See it! Look above the circumstances. Do you see the answer coming? Do you hear it? It is already on its way. See the positive promises of God. It might be small, but it will grow into a full-blown answer. His favor is live. See it! Let your faith arise within you and see it coming. It is yours. Life is in it!

There's a river of life flowing out from me;
Makes the lame to walk and the blind to see.
Opens prison doors sets the captive free;
There's a river of life flowing out from me.

Spring up oh well, within my soul,
Spring up oh well, and make me whole.
Spring up oh well, and give to me
That life abundantly.
—Phil Wickham

Above: Glad Tidings
590 Cambie

Above Right: The Brick
Mason

Right: Good-bye,
Vancouver

Above: Abbotsford
Glad Tidings

Below: Hwy 99 Abby
Glad Tidings

Right: Gospel Mission to Uganda - Youth Club

Above: Gospel Mission to Uganda - Choir

Right: Beacon Light Mission,
Vancouver

Above: Outdoor Meeting

Right: Gospel Mission to Uganda- Safari

Below: Equator

CHAPTER FIVE

And It Came to Pass

Many times folk have asked me: How have you kept going in spite of all you have been through, in so many adventures through the years? It is not very complicated . . . You just don't quit!

> *Christ is enough for me,*
> *Everything I need is in you!*
> *I have decided to follow Jesus,*
> *No turning back, no turning back!*

People today have a problem. We give up! We lose hope, so our faith becomes weak. Everywhere you look, you see a lack of commitment. We move from fad to fad, method to method, and job to job, looking for "pie in the sky."

Even in the Church . . .

- The prophetic word hasn't come to pass . . .
- God's promises (miracles, healing, power, authority)
- Poor me! It is all about me!
- Hard Times.
- We don't agree.

- We don't like . . . the kids' programs, the music, the preaching, the lights, etc.

God Is the Only Sure Hope

> "Now faith is the substance of things hoped for,
> the evidence of things not seen."
> —Hebrews 11:1

In every circumstance by faith, I learned to keep my hope in my Everlasting Father, remembering that I was being led by my Good Shepherd. He was guiding me, and, believe me, many times it took all the faith I could muster up to follow. Thank you, Jesus, for your abundant grace when doubts haunted me.

The strength of *your faith is . . . Where is your hope?*

How will this happen?

For me, there is only one answer. After 80 years of life and 64 years of ministering, I can say, *You Just Don't quit!*

Toronto

As a child, I was scared. The air raid sirens were moaning loud and clear. Mother rushed outside to gather Ruth and me into the house, where we pulled down the shades and waited for the "all clear" sound. I was so frightened. Mother gathered us in her arms and prayed loud and long, and soon it was over.

> "Don't quit, even if it costs you your life (and it will)!
> Stay there believing.
> I have a Life-Crown sized and ready for you.
> Are your ears awake? Listen.
> Listen to the Wind Words (Holy Spirit mighty rushing wind),
> the Spirit blowing through the churches.
> Christ-conquerors are safe from Devil-death."
> —Revelation 2:10, 11 (MSG)

Wiarton

In 1944 I started first grade in a new school in a new town, but I was with my new friend, whom I had just met in my new church: my friend Margaret Inglis, who became my lifelong friend. We prayed together with our pastor to receive Jesus, and we both have served Him all the days of our life, Margaret in Ontario, and me wherever Lew took me in the world! We had the same birthday—June 19, 1938—and behaved like twins, which was not always good. We were in Miss Thiessen's class in 2nd grade, and she gave us both a "bad conduct" on our report card because we could not stop talking. We kept on having fun and messing around. Margaret tells me that when I left she got "good conduct" comments. How could that happen? I was such a fun angel!

Ruth and I had to walk over a mile to town for school, and it was cold, with lots of snow. There was a farmer who drove his horse and sleigh on the snow-packed road outside our house into town every morning, and Ruth and I would catch onto the back of the sleigh, put our feet on the runners, and hold on for dear life—quite the ride. You had to jump off correctly or you had a problem, especially if he sped up so he could dump you. Margaret jumped off first on the way home. It was a contest to see who got dumped, and who landed properly, or who couldn't jump and had to hang on till he slowed down and then walk back! The driver was handicapped and had no arms, so he drove furiously with the reins over his shoulders and with that movement he directed the horses.

One winter Dad decided we would go stay at the farm to celebrate Christmas. I was so excited. I loved the farm. In order to make the experience authentic, he borrowed a horse and buggy from a friend. We and all the gifts were snuggled down into our blankets, moving across the snowy fields and enjoying the crisp air with the snow flying up behind us. It was like a Christmas card, until all of a sudden, Bob (the horse) got a whiff of his home. He dumped us in the snow, presents and all, and took off with the buggy, leaving us in the snow! I remember my Dad running after Bob, yelling, "Bob, come back! Bob, come back!" while Bob just kept going. Dad took after him all the way to the barn. The owner came out and helped us get to our farmhouse. Dad meant well, but he wasn't a seasoned farmer. He was a retired Toronto businessman.

I enjoyed riding on the trailer while Dad drove the tractor. On this particular day Dad was gathering wood, and Ruth and I were riding on top of the wood in the wagon. As we came through the gate, Dad forgot that the barbed wire went over the top of the gate frame. Ruth was sitting down, but I was standing up, thoroughly enjoying the moments, and I didn't see the barbed wire coming at me. Yes, for the rest of my life I have had to explain to every doctor how those scars got there.

Dad loved to tease me about my love for the animals. One summer morning he called me to come because he had something for me. I looked, and he held up a small animal. I ran over to him, thinking it was a new kitty. I had the habit of bringing home stray cats, and they were always delegated to the barn. Anyway, when I got to the barn a great disappointment was in store for me. It was a baby skunk! Dad was delighted that he had fooled me, but I was just sad.

> "Since God has so generously let us in on what he is doing, we're not about to throw up our hands and walk off the job just because we run into occasional hard times."
> —2 Corinthians 4:1 (MSG)

You Just Don't Quit!

Mission City

My Dad had accepted a Pastorate with the PAOC, so my family moved west to British Columbia. This move tore me away from my friends, our church and the farm. I was not happy, but I still felt a measure of anticipation in experiencing the unknown. So, I grudgingly left Margaret and we headed west.

It was a long drive from Ontario to British Columbia. I was amazed as we came into the mountains, as I had never seen a mountain. All I had known were the rolling hills of Ontario. I was especially awestruck by Yellowstone Park and Old Faithful. I was scared as we drove down Hells Gate canyon on a one-way road, where one of the oncoming cars had to back up to find a place to let the other go by.

Finally we came to a little city set on the side of what looked to me like a mountain, overlooking the Fraser Valley. The first Sunday I met my Sunday School teacher, Mr. Kelly—a simple hardware clerk who loved Jesus and loved kids. He became my friend, and the Lord used him to mentor me in the ways of the Lord. He taught me the Bible stories with his creative talent. I remember the manna (puffed oats!) coming down from heaven (a sheet rigged up from the ceiling) to feed the Israelites. He taught me the song of the order of the books of the Bible and challenged me to memorize scripture, which I have used innumerable times over the years when teaching and preaching. He taught me . . .

You Just Don't Quit!

1948 was such a memorable year for me. In early June the Thompson system of rivers, together with the Fraser River, broke through their dykes and the valley flooded. The water went roaring by Mission City, tearing out bridges and swallowing up towns, farmland and animals. Because Mission City was on the side of a hill, it became the refuge for all the towns caught in the flood. I saw my Dad on a long raft, rescuing cows from the roaring torrent, when helping one of the congregation with his herd. The schools farther up the valley had to come to our school, because it was on the hill behind our home and church. We had our classes at the fairgrounds. My mother made a scrapbook of the flood. The amazing pictures show how much water covered the valley. In the end, the rivers rose 14.8 feet above flood stage.

North Battleford, Saskatchewan

In the 1940s many of the Pentecostal pastors were seeking God for a new outpouring of the Holy Spirit. There was such a hunger for more of the Spirit. A Bible training school located in North Battleford, Saskatchewan was holding services in a former Air Force Base building, where the ministries of the laying on of hands and prophecy were being restored. Also, in the past year our congregation had spent an entire year in 24-hour prayer seeking God to move in a new way. We lived under the church on the side of the hill, and I could hear the folk coming into the church to pray at all hours.

Wanting to be certain that what was happening was from God, some of the teachers called the ministry team and the student body to join them in fasting and prayer. The students fasted for three weeks. Prophecy came, announcing a coming revival, and stating that the gifts of the Holy Spirit would be restored and received by the laying on of hands and prophecy. After this, they sent everyone to their dorms to search the Scriptures. When they came back the next day they all pointed to the Scriptures in Timothy, where Paul speaks of Timothy receiving the gifts of the Spirit by the laying on of hands and prophecy. After this, they began to lay hands and prophesy over the students and others. That was February 12, 1948.

News of the outpouring spread like wildfire among the Pentecostals throughout Canada and the United States. In July of 1948, when the news came to Dad, he immediately gathered up Ruth and me, and we headed for North Battleford. Mother had to make a trip east to look after family matters, so I had the privilege of being at the camp meeting and experiencing firsthand the amazing outpouring of the Spirit, with fresh truth for God's people.

At that camp meeting Dad experienced firsthand the outpouring of the Holy Spirit. He saw people receive personal prophetic ministry and the ministry of the laying on of hands to receive the gifts of the Spirit. This encounter with the Holy Spirit at this meeting had a tremendous impact on Dad's life and ministry. Even though I was a 10 year-old child, I can still see the setting and hear the praise and worship that flowed like a river. I was supposed to be in the tent sleeping like a good girl, but I was hiding in the back corner where Dad could not see me listening and watching. When the prophetic word came over my Dad—I will never forget the awesome, overwhelming presence of God.

Vancouver, BC

The summer I turned ten we moved to Vancouver. I want to make sure everyone understands that I was not walking on "cloud nine" through my teen years. I played hooky from school, I loved the boys, I ran track, and I roller skated the sidewalks with the neighborhood kids, but also during that time I was keenly aware of God's hand on my destiny. I understood the powerful presence of God that protected me from danger. His grace picked me up when I stumbled and fell. But my teen foolishness was not what really mattered in those years; it was God's holy presence that overtook my spirit and guided me into my destiny and God's purpose. My Everlasting Father guided my every step. He is my Good Shepherd.

After the meetings were over in North Battleford, Dad asked the leadership to come to his church in Vancouver. This prophetic team ministered personal prophecy and impartation to many believers at the church. Pastors and others also came from different parts of British Columbia and Washington State. These candidates spent at least three days in prayer and fasting to prepare themselves to receive the laying on of hands with prophetic word.

Dad spent the next three months in intense prayer, around four hours daily, asking God to pour out His Spirit mightily on the church and to send more men. He told the Lord, "If men are not coming in, then I'll know it wasn't my call, and I'm going to get out." Dad took the stand that the Holy Spirit had to draw the people to the church, not man's human efforts—and He did. The church grew from 65 people to over 800 on-fire believers. They had more young men in the church than young women.

During the services there were many that testified of hearing a heavenly choir of angels singing. Words of knowledge, spiritual songs, prophetic singing, and the song of the Lord were heard in every service. There were people speaking in unknown tongues and others who heard unfamiliar languages, like Chinese. There was the sound of a pipe organ being beautifully played by a professional organist, when *no such organ existed in the building*. It was just the sound of God's people singing and making melody unto the Lord.

Dad was known for his message on the Sacrifice of Praise, and he became known as the Apostle of Praise. He would preach on the Sacrifice of Praise, then invite the congregation to stand, take his watch off and put it on the pulpit, and say: "We are going to offer a sacrifice of praise for one minute. Lets lift our hands and begin to praise the Lord." The presence of the Lord would descend, and then when the moment was over, Dad would go to stop them. The pastor would beg him not to stop them. He would be so excited that indeed God is enthroned upon the praises of the believer.

I was a pre-teen through the first few years of the Revival, and then through my teen years I experienced such a powerful consciousness of God's presence personally. The revival continued and grew in momentum, and I grew with it. It molded my DNA to this day. I saw it, felt it, experienced it, taught it, and preached it, walking it every day from that day till this day in 2019. The purpose of this writing is not to record all the details of the '48 revival but to let everyone know that it is the foundation of my destiny in God.

"And it came to pass at the end of the four hundred and
thirty years—on that very same day
it came to pass that all the armies of the Lord
went out from the land of Egypt."
—Exodus 12:41

"You have dwelt long enough at this mountain.
Turn and take (set) your journey . . .
see I have set the land before you:

go in and possess the land which the Lord
swore to your fathers . . . to give
to them and their descendants after them."
—Deuteronomy 1:6–8

You Just Don't Quit!

Abbotsford

"We are going to send Dorothy and Velma to Africa, and Lew and Marion Peterson will go to Abbotsford to pastor the church." Dad was speaking on a Sunday morning to the Glad Tidings congregation.

Lew and I looked at each other, our faces full of surprise. That was the first we had heard about this arrangement! We were the ones who wanted to go to Africa. We didn't have a desire or ministry call to Abbotsford.

"Therefore do not be vague and thoughtless and foolish,
but understanding and firmly grasping
what the will of the Lord is."
—Ephesians 5:17

Was this the will of God for our life? I hope so! We had been married nine months, we both had jobs, we had purchased a house—why now? And it wasn't to go to Africa? We had no idea, no inkling at all, and here it was. Pastor? That was our calling, but to Africa, and Uganda was the country of choice. We wanted to join Hugh and Audrey.

Meeting with Dad got us nowhere. "Dad, we don't know about this. We just got married. Is this the right time?"

"You need experience, and you need to get to it. Abbotsford is a small community and you will learn, and in time you will be ready for Uganda."

"How long?

"We don't know, let's see how it goes and how the Lord leads. Go pastor, and let His will be done!"

So we sold the house, I quit my job, we loaded up and were off to Abbotsford to a patient, wonderful group of people. It didn't take long for us to love them, as they allowed us to practice on them. Lew often said we should have paid them, instead of us receiving our $15.00 a week. Lew remained with Nels Peterson and Sons for 8 months.

Lew would drive into Burnaby early in the morning and arrive back in Abbotsford late in the evening. We lived in a rented building on Fraser Highway, then Hwy 99, the Trans Canada Highway. It had no kitchen, no bathroom (except in the church section), no hot water, so no shower, and the rats had their Olympics under the raised floor. The oil heater was on the church side and only lasted half the night. The building was one large room, so they had converted one third of it for our home, and two thirds for the church, separated by a heavy drape that my Mother gave us.

Our daughter Mari Lou was born while we lived there, so then the men of the church put in a hot water tank, and a shower (entrance on the Church side), along with a small counter that we could put our electrical appliances on. That was a glorious day! This made life with the baby somewhat easier. My pregnancies were very hard, and I was very sick. Lew learned to make me tea before I put my feet on the ground.

On his first attempt I said, "Don't forget to heat the pot."

"Okay," so he proceeded to put the Royal Albert china teapot—a wedding present—on the hot plate, to heat the pot!

Of course, that was the end of the teapot. Another lesson.

We still had to go back and forth to the Glad Tidings happenings, as we were in training, and I was still a Pioneer Girls club leader. With only one car, Lew would take me in for the meetings and wait for me. On one of those occasions Lew decided to drop into the PNE grounds for a minute to watch a wrestling match, while Mari Lou slept in the car. He got engrossed in the match. After too long he remembered Mari Lou and raced out to the car in a panic. He threw open the door and grabbed her up. Of course she was terribly frightened, because she was still sound asleep! Lew was relieved because she was still alive! As a new father, he had learned a valuable lesson.

On the way home from Burnaby one night after a hard day on the brick pile, then taking care of some business responsibilities, Lew was stopped for drunk driving. The officer knew him and said, "I know you are not drunk, Reverend. You need to sleep, and if you are this tired, just pull over and take a nap so you will get home safely." And he followed Lew home. Finally Lew sold his partnership to his brother Bob. At last we were in fulltime ministry, but not in Uganda.

Dave and Fran Huebert were part of our congregation, and we became good friends. They were married a week before us and lived in Chilliwack. Every Monday we would meet with them to enjoy dinner together and go to Harrison Hot Springs for a swim and our weekly clean up.

Fran was a teacher and a fine pianist. We were blessed to have her as our pianist, until Dad decided to send them to temporarily pastor the new church plant in Chilliwack. Her mother, Grandma Sperling, did a great job filling in for Fran but it just wasn't the same. The "temporary" assignment stretched out for many years. They pastored Glad Tidings in Chilliwack for many years, laying a solid foundation that is still strong today. I am so thankful for this longtime friendship that continues still today.

After we had been in Abbotsford for over two years, one of the men who owned property offered to give us an acre to build a church building. It was located outside of town, and people thought we were crazy to build a church whose closest neighbors would be cows and a chicken farm across the street. However, we went ahead and built it with living quarters below the auditorium.

Dedication day came January 2, 1961, and Lew was going to be ordained. We were so excited. A huge crowd arrived from Vancouver Glad Tidings to celebrate with us. As they praised and worshiped with all the GT rhythm and enthusiasm, the floor bounced so much that some of the men panicked. All was well until the sewer backed up! Lew changed clothes, and out he went to fix the problem. What a day that was! The ordination was accomplished, and the church was dedicated. One more step closer to Uganda.

"Be anxious for nothing,
but in everything by prayer and supplication
with thanksgiving,
let your requests be made known to God."
—Philippians 4:6

You Just Don't Quit!

Uganda

Dad had a world vision, having been influenced by Oswald J. Smith of The Peoples Church in Toronto. Dad's first Pastor, Daddy Bake, wrote, "Missionary giving has increased our range of usefulness. It has given us a part in the evangelization of the world and thus has enabled us to bear fruit far beyond the range of our local activities. It pushed out the four walls of our assembly to include the uttermost parts of the earth."

Dad was convinced that a church should spend more money on missions than it did operating the church. His passion for missions can be found in this statement: "To me, if you're not doing missionary work, you haven't got a church. If you're spending all your money on the Pentagon at home and sending no soldiers out, you're not getting very far." Dad began a full-time Bible School to train men and women in ministry and to be sent to the nations. Through the ministry of Glad Tidings Missionary Society (GTMS), he fulfilled his passion. The budget for world missions exceeded the budget for the church operation.

During a weeknight service in the winter of 1956, there was a prophetic call for Glad Tidings to send missionaries to Uganda, East

Africa. When Dad applied to the British Governor of Uganda for permission to enter the country to do missions work, the application was refused, because the Archbishop of the Anglican Church did not want another mission in Uganda. Undaunted, Dad believed this call was of God. The church began to pray fervently for God to open the door. That was the year I graduated from high school and entered Vancouver Vocational Institute to please my Mom, who wanted me to have a career other than ministry. Believe me, I was praying fervently for Uganda!

In December 1956, GTMS sent Hugh and Audrey to Kenya to work with the Elim missionaries of New York until the door opened to Uganda. That door opened in May 1960, enabling Hugh and Audrey to move to Uganda, opening the door for the Gospel message, which spread like a fire across the country. Thus began a great and powerful move of God that continues today, with thousands of believers attending hundreds of churches, with numerous associations from around the world.

During Dad's time of pastoring in Vancouver, GTMS sent out some 44 missionaries, all with a mighty zeal for the Lord to reach the lost and pioneer new churches. He didn't believe in bringing missionaries back home to collect money so they could continue their mission. He believed that when the church sent out missionaries it should make sure their needs were met as long as they were on the field. In order to support this vision, he urged the congregation to give a double tithe: 10 percent to the church and 10 percent to missions, which we all gave, excited to be a part of God's love for the world. I believe that Dad joined the Apostle Paul in saying:

"I have fought the good fight,
I have finished the race,
I have kept the faith.
Finally there is set up for me the crown of righteousness
which the Lord, the righteous Judge,

will give to me on that Day,
and not to me only but also
to all who have loved His appearing."
—2 Timothy 3:7, 8

Presbytery services, October, 1963: "In one year's time you will plant your feet in the land of your calling," Pastor David Schoch had prophesied. Now it was our turn. I was ordained just before we left Vancouver for Uganda on July 23, 1964. Uganda, here we come!

We traveled by train across Canada to Halifax, and then by Norwegian freighter around the Cape and up the coast of Africa. Hugh and Audrey met us at Tanga, Tanzania. It was a amazing trip—21 days without seeing land. Mari Lou turned five on board. We crossed the equator, and in that ceremony we ate raw fish. In Mozambique Lew discovered that "Jambo" wasn't "Jumbo." Not "big," but, "Hello."

Our first night was in Africa was in Mombasa, Kenya. As we were going to bed, Lew spotted a lizard on the wall. He grabbed his shoe, stood on the couch, and tried to kill it, thinking he was defending us. Hugh heard the commotion and came to see what was happening. He laughed at Lew and said, "That's a gecko. We don't kill them—they eat the mosquitoes!" Poor Lew. He was mortified, but then, we were in Africa and had a lot to learn.

October 1964: we had arrived. We were in Uganda at last—a dream come true. A year had passed since Pastor Schoch's prophecy, and we were standing on Uganda's red soil.

The welcome by the believers was overwhelming, beyond anything we could have imagined. "Thank you, Jesus, for this unbelievable opportunity to serve You." Wonderful Jesus!

We moved in to live with one of the missionaries till we got settled, and with a little adjustment we learned to live with the bugs, potential thieves, heat and humidity. But we loved the people, and the zeal of the believers, and easily made lifelong friendships. Before we realized it we were involved with the day-to-day happenings and loving every minute of it!

My niece Ruth was born just after we arrived. What a honor and joy it was to be asked to dedicate her in Makerere Full Gospel Church, Uganda. The memory of that day has never left me. I felt such a deep conviction that she would be used mightily of the Lord in Uganda, as well as in other countries. Her destiny was marked, and the congregation joined me as we prayed that God's anointing, grace and unction would keep her and guide her into the fulfillment of His purpose for her life.

> "In everything give thanks; for this is the will of
> God in Christ Jesus for you."
> —1 Thessalonians 5:18

Vancouver

Dad arrived in Uganda for a visit and said, "Lew and Marion, I need to take you home with me when I leave Uganda this time. I need your help in the church in Vancouver. You will become our Assistant Pastors."

Here we go again. We had never thought about going back to Canada on a permanent basis. As far as we were concerned, we were in Uganda for the rest of our lives. Our plan was to die and be buried in Uganda. This was our calling, and we loved it!

However, it seemed we had no choice, so we packed up once again and travelled home with Dad. We moved into the home that I was raised in, were given a Sunday School room as an office, and settled into pastoring the congregation that we had grown up in. A big change for them, and for us!

Our first responsibility was building, administrating and running the Youth Camps, then building a gymnasium addition onto the present building, with apartments above into which we eventually moved. The location of the church was deteriorating, and one morning when I went to get in my car, which was parked in the carport behind the church, I found a young man in it trying to take out my stereo. Wires were everywhere. I looked at him and said, "What are you doing?"

"Stealing your stereo."

"What are you doing that for?"

"Because I want it. I don't have one."

I couldn't see anyone around to yell for help, so I said, "That is my stereo. Leave it right where it is." I grabbed his arm and tried to stop him, but he tore out my stereo and bolted, running down the lane. I saw a neighbor in his backyard and yelled, "Stop him. He is a thief." No result! That was the end of my stereo, and I suddenly realized what I had done. I raced up to the church office, telling them what happened, and receive a stern reprimand for even talking to the man. I could have been hurt. Thank you, my Everlasting Father, for protection, even in my lack of thought and wisdom.

Sirens? Stopping below our window? What? A fire so close? Smoke was billowing up past our window now. Lew flew out of bed, raced down the hall while dressing, flew down the stairs, and sure enough, smoke was coming out of the church. By the time I got myself together, my heart was racing and I tumbled down the stairs, falling into the arms of one of our friends, as he assured me, "Everything is okay. The fellowship hall and prayer room were damaged, but the fire doors to the auditorium did their job." Then my heart began to beat normally again. I have always been afraid of fire. I checked every house we were moving into to figure out how we could get out in case of a fire. This was too close for me.

You Just Don't Quit!

Travel: USA

Another new experience for us: itinerating and holding meetings, by pulling a 5th wheel mobile home with a big pickup truck. Once we were stuck in the mud in Yuba City, California at Mom and Dad's home, after driving over the mountains near Shasta in a snowstorm.

We were crossing the Tennessee mountains in June, and it began to snow heavily. At the summit, as we began the descent on a road of fresh-fallen snow, with that huge 5th wheel pushing us from behind—talk about prayer! Fortunately, Lew was used to heavy trailers of brick behind him, but I was not. In such emergencies, I find praying in the Holy Spirit helps my nerves, so I did, and out loud. We made it, and found the church on time. What a relief.

It was late, dark and foggy. We were in a hurry to get to the next meeting on time and had only a couple of days to get there. When we finally found the freeway and took the on-ramp, we were going the wrong way! Yes, we had driven down the exit ramp instead of the on-ramp, and our faithful 5th wheel was right behind us. Lew made a quick stop and began to back up the ramp. Now, I don't like to back up at the best of times, but certainly not with a 5th wheel motor home leading the way. Prayer time again.

I had an interesting personal experience in Long Beach, California. We had been with Bethany Chapel for Presbytery meetings. Before we left California we went browsing in the mall together. Lew and I were walking with Pastor Schoch, and Mom and Dad were behind us with Audene.

David asked me, "Are you really delivered from GT?"

I laughed, and said, "Yes, we are on our own now."

"Okay, prove it."

He marched me into the closest jewelry store and said to the clerk, "This lady wants her ears pierced. I gasped and looked at Lew. He smiled and shrugged his shoulders. Then I looked around for my Dad, who was outside the store talking. The lady sat me down and pierced my ears. Earrings? Oh, help! What will Dad say? Nothing! I guessed that he had given up on me, his rebellious child, now 40 years of age.

Our next ministry stop was in Texas. We pulled into the church driveway to park our 5th wheel, met the Pastor, and settled in for the night. First thing in the morning there came a knock on the door. It was the Pastor, who said to Lew: "Can I talk with you for a moment?"

"Sure, come on in."

He hesitated, then stepped inside looking at me. I settled them together with a cup of coffee.

Pastor said, "I assume you and your wife minister together on the platform?"

"Yes," Lew answered. "That is right."

"I also noticed she wears earrings."

"Yes, she does."

"Well, she cannot come on the platform wearing earrings."

Without a blink, Lew said, "That is no problem, she just won't wear them."

The Pastor smiled. "Okay, that is fine. See you both in the service." And then he left.

I looked at Lew and said, " I can't take these earrings out. My ears have to heal first. I will just not minister today."

Lew said, " No, we have to do this. We will comply with their rules. You will minister with me as usual." And I did just that.

After the service we went back to our 5th wheel and Lew proceeded to help me put the earrings back in, since my ears were very sore and touchy. In the process he dropped one down the drain! Lew looked just devastated. What now? The trap. We took the drain apart and rescued the earring, and proceeded with the job at hand. Lew wondered, "Was this judgment from God?" but came to the conclusion that if Isaac's Rebecca could receive a gift of earrings from Isaac, then Marion can have earrings received from the prophet of God. Another lesson learned. God's Grace is sufficient!

I was glad when the itinerary ministry was over. For me it was difficult in every way. The 5th wheel just didn't cut it for me. I am a nester, both naturally with my home, and spiritually with my church and the people in it. We needed to settle again, and pastor. That was our call and our love. God's ways are not our ways, but He does know the desire of our hearts, so we stepped into the next season.

You Just Don't Quit!

Yuba City, California

Settling in Yuba City was a cultural shock. The congregation was made up of mostly ex-hippies, and now Jesus People, who were willing to be taught and become a part of an organized local church. They accepted us, and our traditional ways, with graciousness and love. We preached the message that we had burning in our souls, and they accepted and entered into all that the Lord had for them. There were some tragedies, but the majority received the word and have continued moving on in God's purposes for their lives still today.

We made so many wonderful friends, and the youth became like sons and daughters to us. We found the summer weather to be extremely hot and uncomfortable. You could fry an egg on the sidewalk. During that time all four of our parents went to heaven. Mari Lou met and married Jeffery Holmes. We bought a small house, then sold it and bought a mobile home, moving it onto Mom and Dad's property so we could be near them. After Mom and Dad passed, we moved it into a trailer park, then eventually sold it.

Lew helped the young people and built the new brick church. I started an ACE school, with grades 1 through 12. We gathered a fellowship of pastors from the Sacramento Valley and enjoyed the various talents of these awesome young people. We learned to harvest walnuts and enjoyed the abundant fruit and veggies from the farms around us.

We were learning a culture other than the one we grew up in. Still, we continually felt the tug of Uganda in our souls, dreaming that one day we would see that land again. I can't say I enjoyed everything that came my way in this learning curve, but with Paul I can say:

> "But none of these things move me;
> nor do I count my life dear to myself,
> so that I may finish my race with joy,
> and the ministry which I received from the Lord Jesus,

to testify to the gospel of the grace of God."
—Acts 20:24

Uganda, Again

"What do you think?" Lew asked, as we flew back to Yuba City from Uganda.

" You first!" I replied.

Looking apprehensive, he replied, "I told Joshua we would come back to help."

"I agree," was my reply.

God had spoken to both of us while on our visit in Uganda. The country and the church were struggling and devastated. We began to discuss all the scenarios, if we did return.

We returned to Yuba City, discussed it with Mari Lou and Jeff, and the Tices, and made ready to return to Uganda. That meant traveling again to raise the necessary funds to fulfill the vision.

RUN Ministries

Lew had chosen RUN Ministries, "Restore Uganda Now" as the name of our ministry, because we felt the need to encourage and strengthen the pastors. We had no desire to start another mission, but would work together with the Full Gospel Churches of Uganda, the mission Hugh and Audrey had founded in 1960 when we had ministered together with them in the '60s.

We began traveling to raise our support. The response was fantastic, and we were very encouraged. On our way back to Yuba City on Christmas Eve 1984 with a very loaded car, we hit black ice and the car turned over, pinning both of us under the dash. Lew got out through the window hole first, and I followed. A kind man came along in a warm pickup that I sat in, saving me from shock, until the police and ambulance came. In the hospital, the emergency nurse said she had been praying for whom she did not know, but obviously it was us. They sent us home, for me to see my doctor and have my shoulder screwed together.

We had our carload of gifts, I was incapacitated, and we were travelling without suitcases. All by himself Lew had to pack up everything in boxes, get it all on the plane to Salem, take a bus to Portland and another plane to San Francisco to meet Mari Lou and Jeff, and then home with broken me. It was quite an undertaking. After my surgery, we went to the Revival Fellowship Conference and heard the prophetic word: "You go to do one thing; I send you to do another. Through the midst of confusion and ploy for power, I will fulfill my purpose!" Ah, my Shepherd.

To God be the glory, great things He hath done.
So loved He the world that He gave us His Son.
Who yielded His life an atonement for sin,
And opened the life gate that all may go in.

Praise the Lord, praise the Lord,
Let the earth hear His voice.
Praise the Lord, praise the Lord, Let the people rejoice!
O, come to the Father, through Jesus, the Son,
And give Him the glory, great things He hath done.

O, perfect redemption, the purchase of blood,
To every believer the promise of God.
The vilest offender who truly believes,
That moment from Jesus a pardon receives.
—Fanny Crosby (1875)

It hasn't always been easy, but we never stopped learning to trust. Thank you, Andre, for your musical expression of what it is like putting one step in front of another, as we move toward our final destiny. We spent the next 13 more years in Uganda fulfilling God's plan for our destiny. I like to think those years were the "cherry on top of the cake" years—the best years of our lives and ministry. I really believe God arranged it that way. We were spent when it was over, and I have recorded those adventures in Chapter 7, "80 Years By Faith". Lew made it to heaven before me, but I will follow when I am done.

What a fellowship, what a joy divine,
Leaning on the everlasting arms.
What a blessedness, what a peace is mine,
Leaning on the everlasting arms.

Leaning, leaning, safe and secure from all alarms;
Leaning, leaning, leaning on the everlasting arms.

What have I to dread, what have I to fear,
Leaning on the everlasting arms?
I have blessed peace with my Lord so near,
Leaning on the everlasting arms.

—E. A. Hoffman (1887)

You Just Don't Quit!

Portland, OR

We were home to stay. It was time. We bought a home in Gresham. Mari Lou and Jeff, and Edward and Brian were nearby, and we were enjoying being close to each other at last. Basketball was the game, and we loved going to their games—or should I say learning the game? Ed was "Holmes" and Brian was "Little Holmes." They were so much fun. Jeff was such a good father and his boys respected his wisdom. Mari Lou was the best mother, and as an exceptional councilor she loves her boys unconditionally and serves her family with great joy.

We enjoyed our times together. I loved having a home so that the grandsons could stop by anytime to visit and raid the cookie jar. Christmas, Thanksgiving, Easter and Birthdays were special times that we could now celebrate together. At one of these occasions Brian was a little "antsy" and had been excused from the dinner table. In the process, he knocked over my little cup and saucer stand, which I shouldn't have had sitting on a side table anyway. Jeff rose to the occasion and reprimanded Brian. I said, "Don't worry, it's okay. It doesn't matter," and got up to pick up the pieces. The look on Mari Lou's face was priceless. Is that my mother? If that had been me, I would have been in big trouble. So is the response of the Grandma!

The grandsons changed my life. Stuff happens, and the grandsons made me realize I didn't have to prove anything or impress anyone. I just wanted to show them my love. Stuff can be replaced, so why make an issue over stuff? I guess we all come to that place, where if we could do parenting over again we would do it differently. That is where I had come to.

Lew became a staff Pastor at City Bible Church in Portland. The preaching days were pretty well over for both of us. We introduced LewMar Ministries and traveled a bit, making missions trips to different countries, loved the prophetic assemblies we participated in, and the teaching times, but ministry life had certainly slowed down for us. Lew was part of the apostolic team for MFI for a season, which kept him attached to the African churches.

To help with our income for a season, I worked for the Oregon Building Department as an Administrative Assistant. It was a political situation and soon became difficult to endure. I received an invitation from the California Education Network to assist them with producing curriculum for their Charter Schools, supervising the writers and receiving their manuscripts through the internet, then passing them on to the head office in California to be printed and distributed. I took the job so I could work at home and enjoyed it till the curriculum was pretty well done. Then they wanted me to move to California and handle the distribution, with Lew as the school's chaplain. We did not want to move, so I sadly resigned. By that time we were traveling more, but Lew was showing signs of progression in his disease, and when we traveled the responsibilities and decisions fell more and more to me. What to do?

You Just Don't Quit!

Chehalis / Centralia, Washington

"Why don't you guys move here to be in our church, instead of just dropping in once in a while?" asked Pastor Derrill Corbin.

" We have thought about it," we answered. "Are you sure? At our age, would that be a good idea?"

"Of course," he replied. "We need some older people here with us to help guide the younger. A little experience would be an asset to Life Center."

We moved into Chehalis, built our dream home, then lost it in the recession, and moved to a Senior Living Community in Centralia. I went to work at Walmart, then substituted in the Centralia School District, trying to find our way financially.

We rehearsed His promises. We don't quit. We turn and continue our journey, and look back with no regrets, joyful that we are still on His journey in every season. We had changed, and our life had changed, but we had not quit. The Bible is full of people who didn't quit. Were they perfect? No! Mistakes? Yes! God gives us choices at the crossroads, then He guides us in each step.

We were ready to turn and reset our journey, to let our faith arise stronger than ever before, because we will not quit the journey. We will see the next generation become as set in the hope as we had enjoying his marvelous grace, led by the Shepherd. After all, He still is the Everlasting Father.

"So we are not giving up. How could we?
Even though on the outside it often looks like
things are falling apart on us,
on the inside, where God is making new life,
not a day goes by without his unfolding grace.
These hard times are small potatoes compared to
the coming good times, the lavish celebration prepared for us.
There is far more here than meets the eye.
The things we see now are here today, gone tomorrow,
but the things we can't see now will last forever."
—2 Corinthians 4:16 (MSG)

We are Christ conquerors!

Return to Canada

"Welcome Home, Lew and Marion," was what we heard over and over again. Open arms held us as we cried happy tears and felt big hugs. After being away from Canada for almost 40 years, we didn't know what to expect, and it turned out to be a big party day. So many of our longtime friends stood there smiling and loving on us. They presented us with the finances to purchase a car, including the first year of servicing and gas! We were overwhelmed, and oh, so grateful. It was a new season with longtime friends at our side to begin once again.

You Just Don't Quit!

We needed His Redeeming Grace to be demonstrated to our world in every season. He led us a step at a time through all the adventures. Some we planned, but most we didn't. We found He was certainly our Good Shepherd. Yes, he had his rod that prodded us along, but it was certainly comforting to know He was with us continually, urging us along.

"The Lord is my Shepherd, I shall not want.
He leads me in the paths of righteousness for His name's sake.
I will fear no evil, for you are with me,
Your rod and your staff they comfort me."
Psalm 23:1–4

Left: Wedding Cake

Right: First Anniversary

Below: Gospel Mission to Uganda - Missionaries

Left: Building the Bible College

Below Left: Gospel Mission to Uganda - Mom's Visit

Below: Opening Bible College

Left: City Bible Church Lay Pastors & Lew Peterson

Right: City Bible Church, Ladies Mentor Group

Left: 25th Anniversary

Right: 50th Anniversary

Left: Signing,
It's Still the Cross

CHAPTER SIX

They're Coming!

*A*s Betty grabbed me and pulled me out the door of the shop, my purchases hit the ground. "Marion, we have to get out of here!" Betty said anxiously.

"Why?" I asked.

"They're coming," she answered.

"Who's coming?" I asked.

"I don't know, we just have to GO!" she yelled.

I assumed our shopping day was done as we joined the huge mass of people moving out of Kampala. If you can imagine, there I was, a very white, old lady, trying to run uphill amongst a massive, jostling crowd. Everyone was yelling, crying, and moving in a hurry. Merchandise was being hauled inside while shops were being closed—it was mass confusion. People were running around the cars, busses, taxis, and trucks, all blocking the way out. Every road was blocked. Breathing heavily we moved up toward Kampala Road.

"Where are we going?" I asked.

"Out of downtown, away from Kampala Road," She answered.

We stopped at her friend's café. As she was hurriedly closing down, she suggested we go to her house up on Nakasero hill.

"No," I said. "If we are going anywhere, let's go to the church, because that is where Lew will come looking for me."

Betty agreed. "Okay," she said. They were obviously anxious about the safety of this white woman if a coup was in progress. So we took off running, down into the valley, through the trees full of sleeping bats, up the hill, through the small village, up another hill, and finally I collapsed on the grass beside Makerere Full Gospel Church, hoping that my guess was correct and Lew would come there, expecting to find me. After a bit of a wait, he came by foot. We were so happy that we were both safe, yet still, none of us knew why?

"Where is the pickup?" I asked.

He laughed, "In the garage."

"Why didn't you come with it?" I asked, "That is a long walk with four roadblocks along the way, and you are white and defenseless!"

Laughing, he said, "I was at home when one of the neighbors came running to tell us there was a riot in town, and everyone was running to escape. I knew you were with Betty in town and that they would do everything they could to protect you. So I jumped in the truck and headed for town. When I got down to the main road, I turned toward Kampala, driving as fast as I dared. I was going to find you. Up ahead I saw this mass of vehicles as wide as the road racing towards me, so I made a quick U-turn and went home. I put the truck in the garage, took out the router, and locked all the doors and gates. I figured that Betty would get you to the church, so if I was going to find you, I had to walk, and here you are, and here I am. Thank you, Jesus!"

Someone from the church took us home, and all was well there. We never did find out who was coming. Our adventure was over for that day.

Hakuna Mutata — "No Worries"

"Therefore do not worry about tomorrow,
for tomorrow will worry about his own things.

Sufficient for the day is its own trouble."
—Matthew 6:34

"Be anxious for nothing, but in everything
by prayer and supplications
with thanksgiving,
let your requests be made known to God;
and the peace of God,
which surpasses all understanding,
will guard your hearts and minds through Christ Jesus."
—Philippians 4:6–7

Stuff happens. In all our lives we experience things that we didn't expect or plan. I don't do as well with the unplanned events. I like my ducks all in a row, with lists made, and in accomplishment order. When I pick up my friends to do errands with me, I have a sticky note on the dash with the order in which I am going to do the errands. I like to plan everything well ahead of time, but as life went on I had to learn to be spontaneous. At times I surprised myself at how well I did, and other times I was totally ashamed of my reaction. To respond is to have had time to think it through and then do the correct thing. To react is off the cuff. BLAH! And then, for me, that often ends up requiring an apology.

He has me covered. His banner over me is *His Love!* Even with my mistakes He still loves me and reaches out to help me. When it was my fault and I didn't handle the situation correctly, He was still there with his unconditional love to pick me up and show the way. God said King David was a man after his own heart, and yet we know David's reactions were not always correct. In fact, he made some bad decisions that were written down so all the world could know. But then we read Psalm 51, and we understand why God loved him, even though, without thinking he reacted wrongly, and he really messed up in a touchy situation. But the way he responded to the prophet made him a man after God's heart. "Oh my, I am that man," he said. "Oh God, I'm so sorry."

"Create in me a clean heart, O God,
and renew a steadfast spirit within me.
Do not cast me away from Your presence,
and do not take Your Holy Spirit from me.
Restore to me the joy of Your salvation,
and uphold me by Your generous Spirit.
Then I will teach transgressors your ways,
and sinners shall be converted to You."
—Psalm 51:10–13

It boils down to what Jesus accomplished on the cross. His blood cleanses all our booboos, all our sins, all our indiscretions. All we have to do is confess, accept his promises, and believe.

My Savior's Love

It was 1966, and it was choir practice night in Uganda. We were under a curfew because of the coup, but it was hard to leave Makerere Full Gospel Church that night. We had learned a new song (the words are below), and the presence of the Lord was so precious that no one wanted to leave. This song expressed the heart of most everyone in the choir. Our star bass was a middle-aged man with a fabulous voice. He was married with 4 or 5 children, and had become a wonderful husband and father since giving his life to Jesus. Before that he was a drunkard and spent most of his time and money in the local bar near his home.

Everyone left the church quickly because of the curfew, since we had stayed late. This new song was Kyakuleese's heart. As he rode his bicycle home, he sang the new song he had just learned. It so expressed how grateful he was for his salvation. As he passed the old bar he was singing:

How marvelous, how wonderful,
and my song shall ever be

How marvelous, how wonderful
is my Savior's love for me.

I stand amazed in the presence of Jesus the Nazarene,
And wonder how He could love me,
a sinner condemned, unclean.

For me it was in the garden, He prayed:
"Not My will, but Thine."
He had no tears for His own grief,
but sweat drops of blood for mine.

In pity angels beheld Him, and came from
the world of light
To comfort Him in the sorrows he bore
for my soul that night.

He took my sins and my sorrows;
He made them His very own.
He bore the burden to Calvary and
suffered and died alone.

When with the ransomed in glory,
His face I at last shall see,
'Twill be my joy thru the ages to sing of His love for me.

How marvelous, how wonderful,
and my song shall ever be.
How marvelous, how wonderful is
my Savior's love for me.

—Charles H Gabriel (1905)

Someone jumped him, and he was found the next morning, his throat slit from ear to ear. Still today I am moved when I remember how his death affected us all. They said his old friends were angry with him, or it could have been just thieves. Our solace was that he now saw His face!

These unexpected trials are hard, but His grace is sufficient. Sometimes it is hard to realize that we are in a battle, and enemies will attack. The world, the flesh and the devil are out to get us, but ". . . greater is He that is in us than he that is in the world," even when circumstances don't turn out the way would like them to. He is still the Mighty God, and His banner over us is Love. Suffering, hardships and disappointments never negate His power.

Early in our marriage I miscarried our son. It was traumatic and resulted in an ambulance trip to the hospital. I was close to death. Afterwards they said we wouldn't be able to have any more babies. Then, to defy all the negatives Mari Lou came along 16 months after the trauma. Our beautiful little girl blessed our family, which up to that time had had only boys. Today she is a powerful woman of God, and has raised two sons whose lives are totally sold out for Jesus and His church. Together she and her husband are known for their godly wisdom and counsel. You never know what God will do if we let him guide us and do what is right.

Israel's God-fearing judge Deborah became tired of the enemy's oppression. Village life had ceased. The highways were deserted and Israel was terrified. It was enough. Jabin, King of Canaan, and his Army Commander, Sisera, were technically stronger that Deborah and Barak, her army Commander. Judge Deborah called Barak and instructed him to gather the army, telling him that they were going to war, and would defeat King Jabin.

They went to war, and as Israel was winning, Sisera left his chariot and ran. Barak continued the fight and pursued Sisera's army, and not a man was left standing. Sisera was on foot, and came upon a compound where a woman named Jael lived. She greeted him, as she was the wife of Heber the Kenite, who was at peace with King Jabin. So they kind of knew each other through her husband.

Jael invited Sisera in to rest and covered him with a blanket. He asked for water, and she gave him milk instead to make him relaxed and sleepy. She had a plan. Sisera told her to lie. "If anyone comes by and asks, "Is there any man here?" say, "No." When he was asleep, Jael took a tent peg and a hammer and pinned him through the head to the ground. Soon, Barak came along looking for Sisera, and she said, "Come, I will show you the man whom you seek." And there lay Sisera, dead, with the peg through his temple.

> "So on that day God subdued Jabin king of Canaan
> in the presence of the children of Israel.
> And the hand of the children of Israel
> grew stronger and stronger
> against Jabin King of Canaan,
> until they had destroyed Jabin king of Canaan."
> —Judges 4:23–24

Who would have thought Jael would do something like that? Certainly not Sisera! Yes, the enemy does his thing, but God shows his strong hand through His people, if they listen to the prompting of His Spirit.

Time after time in our journey we faced unexpected battles in so many different ways. Choices had to be made on how to handle them to keep our sanity and safety, while remaining joyful in our calling.

Stuff Happens

We began our ministry in Abbotsford with some odd-ball things that were new to us. We heated the church building, including our home, with a kerosene heater. We had a barrel out back that was filled commercially with kerosene, and we would fill a can to bring it in to the heater. The Evanses from California were visiting us, and their little girl discovered the barrel and the can, and one day she came running to tell her mom that she had turned on the water and couldn't turn it off. We ran to see, and fortunately she hadn't drunk any of it, but it was running down the hill behind our place!

When we built our own building it seemed that we lived with skunks all around us, and their perfume is potent. My friend and neighbor Lois used to vacuum with a deodorant to try to combat the smell surrounding the neighbourhood. They had them under their house. What an interesting life for a city girl. Along with the chicken farm across the street, the perfume was strong daily.

Lew's parents owned a small house trailer, and they would come out to visit and stay a while. One time when they were parked in the driveway, Mom and Dad were resting. Lew was working that day laying bricks somewhere, and suddenly there was a loud boom. The explosion sent me running. I guess Mom had left a gas burner on. She woke up, went to heat water for tea, and blew the trailer up! She was quite badly burned and had to be attended to at the hospital. She healed and was fine.

That battle ended with the insurance company writing it off, and Lew took it and repaired it, and we ended up with a camping trailer ourselves. Amazing!

In order to keep myself from becoming negative after these different challenges, I learned to take them and watch what God would do in the aftermath. Most times there seemed to be an advantage in the end. I loved to read Job in those times, as it caused my faith and hope to rise, as well as my thankfulness for God's mercy and grace.

I did a lot of spiritual warfare through prayer and declaration. Psalm 68 is one of our favorite Psalms. It inspired us to claim God's good hand in all things.

The flood in Centralia was one of those times. Ten feet of water swept over the freeway, and four feet flooded the church building that recently had been so nicely renovated. We had given our books to the church for a library, as well as our large pieces of memorabilia from Uganda to be use for missions displays. All of that was washed away or damaged and had to be destroyed.

Sometimes, like Judge Deborah, we just need a Warrior Spirit to arise and denounce the enemy. We need to sharpen our weapons, practice with them, and learn how to fight effectively. Become an active soldier by enduring hardships, and not become so entangled with the affairs of this life that we put God's ways on the back burner. We must learn to war in the Spirit realm. God, teach my hands to war with the prophetic word, in faith.

"Let God arise." Or, as the Message Bible puts it, "Up with God." How often in life we find ourselves placing more focus on the problem than the "Problem Solver." Our God is a warrior, and He never loses. It is easy in life to turn molehills into mountains unless we understand who He is. Sometimes it seems that He is far from me, and the circumstances of my life are "closing in on me." So... now what? It almost sounds too simple. *Expect God to arise!*

Give Him the permission to come to your defense. Lift Him up, put Him on display, and make Him known in spite of the circumstances, however real they might seem to be. Be proud of your Almighty God.

When He arises, His enemies will be scattered. They will flee before Him, like smoke in the wind, like wax on the fire. What a comforting picture as we see God arising. See the enemy blown away, see his devices melting like wax in His presence. It does not matter what the challenge or problem might be. When God arises, it is gone! More importantly, God is with us, in us and for us. Our enemy is His enemy. The powers of darkness are simply smoke in His presence, melting like wax before His awesome glory.

Trust and Obey

Everyone in the world wants to be happy, but as we have progressed through our lives we have discovered that happiness depends upon our own attitude toward the circumstances in our seasons of life.

When we walk with the Lord in the light of his word,
What a glory He sheds on our way!
While we do His good will He abides with us still,
And with all who will trust and obey.

Not a shadow can rise, not a cloud in the skies,
But His smile quickly drives it away.
Not a doubt nor a fear, not a sign nor a tear,
Can abide while we trust and obey.

But we never can prove the delights of His love
Until all on the altar we lay;
For the favor he shows, and the joy be bestows
Are for those who will trust and obey.

Then in fellowship sweet we will sit at His feet,
Or we'll walk by His side in the way;
What He says we will do, where he sends we will go.
Never fear, only trust and obey.

Trust and obey, for there's no other way
to be happy in Jesus, but to trust and obey.

—John H. Sammis (1887)

In our adult lives Lew and I had very few problems with obedience. We were brought up by Godly parents and leaders (both natural and spiritual) who trained us in obedience to God and others. But trust has been a different challenge!

We knew we were trustworthy, but at times we found ourselves in trouble because we assumed everyone we had dealings with through the years was also as trustworthy. We discovered that some were not.

This presented a challenging problem. It is difficult when you have trusted a circumstance, a person, a government, some church leaders, or even our economy, and then the whole thing falls apart, leaving us with our mouths hanging open in amazement. King David had this problem.

> "Desperadoes have ganged up on me,
>   they're hiding in ambush for me.
> I did nothing to deserve this God,
>   crossed no one, wronged no one.
> All the same, they're after me, determined to get me."
> —Psalm 59:3–4 (MSG)

We remember crying out, "Oh God, what has happened here?"

When a first-time mother lay unconscious, with her young husband watching her being put into the ambulance, crying, "That's my wife."

When a young, godly father of three was killed by a drunk teen running a red light.

When in Africa we didn't have the finances to finish the building needed to hold the pastors that were coming for training.

When the guns were ruling our lives.

More recently, where do we go from here?

And God said, *"You can trust Me."*

Yes, we can (must) trust Him, just like we have done before. He still has His plan for us, even when we feel our trust is weak. We will rise up and say, "I will trust You." And from exercising that trust will come the joy and contentment that we seek after.

> *"Instead of bemoaning the loss of your comfort,*
>   *accept the challenge of something new.*
> *'I lead you from glory to glory, making*
>   *you fit for My Kingdom.'"*
> —*Sarah Young*

- Commence, start with excitement
- Continue, work through in labor
- Completion, enter into rest.

> "Therefore we also, since we are surrounded
> by so great a cloud of witnesses,
> let us lay aside every weight,
> and the sin which so easily ensnares us,
> and let us run with endurance the race that is set before us,
> looking unto Jesus,
> the author and finisher of our faith,
> who for the joy that was set before Him
> endured the cross, despising the shame,
> and has sat down in the right hand of the throne of God."
> —Hebrews 12:1

Weapons

It is time to check our weapons. In a time when "it is all about me", the more that is believed the bigger mess we get into. Declaring our position in Christ, trusting His ways, requires spiritual weapons in good condition. First we need to remember:

> "The weapons of our warfare are not carnal,
> but mighty through God."
> —1 Corinthians 10:4

God gave us a divine strategy that astounded the enemy. God can take what is a little thing and magnify it. We learned not to belittle the weapons God placed in our hands at the times we needed to go to war: a smile, a laugh, prophetic confidence, a helping hand, or perseverance. So many practical weapons influenced the enemy to go back, and God increased them when we lifted Him up.

Reasoning, arguments, bribes, intimidation, retaliation, worry, doubt, guilt or unforgiveness are carnal weapons that will do no good in a battle.

- David wrestled with a sling shot and five stones
- Gideon wrestled with pictures, lamps and trumpets
- Jehosaphat wrestled with a choir and orchestra

Our Weapons:

- The Name of Jesus: our power of attorney to cast out devils and declaring healing
- The Blood of Jesus: When the blood that Christ shed on the Cross is applied to my life, there is both protection and salvation.
- God's Word: When God wants something supernatural to occur in your life, He will speak through His word to your spirit. He will give you exactly what you need at that moment.
- Prayer: God not only hears your prayer, He answers. Don't be impatient. Nothing can be a substitute for persistent prayer.
- Faith: You don't need more faith. Just use what you already have.
- Love: Kill them with kindness! Let love win your battles. Shower your enemies with the Father's love. They will become your friends.
- The Fear of the Lord: The Lord deserves our respect, reverence, worship and fellowship.
- Divine Covenant: You can build a fortress of protection for your life when you come into a covenant relationship with the Lord.

We learned to make the choice to rejoice in the pain, see and believe, learn how to use our spiritual weapons, and triumph in conflict. We had to choose to fight and win. We began to ask God for a vision of what was ahead, and knowing that there would be a battle, how he wanted us to handle it. Winning armies are prepared and have a strategy.

Some battles are harder than others, and some are longer. When we were building the church in Yuba City, one of the girls was up on the roof and she fell through a skylight hole. I don't remember what her injuries were, but it scared us half to death. Why was she up there? Why wasn't the hole covered until the glass came? Who was supervising? We really beat ourselves up over that one.

We made a trip to Tanzania by boat on Lake Victoria, from Kampala to Mwanza. Lew had reserved a state room for us. When we got on board we discovered the stateroom had four bunk beds, all eight beds were full, and all the passengers were men except me. We arrived safely in spite of the accommodation.

Youth Camp here we come. We had driven for hours to get to this camp site, because the vehicle had a leak in the radiator. We had to stop repeatedly when we saw some water, in order that we could scoop it up to keep going. We arrived late, and it was after dark. We were exhausted and just fell into bed. The bugs chirped all night, and Lew was up early to go to prayer.

When I awoke it was light, and the bugs were still chirping but much louder. When my eyes finally opened I discovered where the sound that I heard was coming from. Baby bats were welcoming the adult bats home from the night's hunt. We were living with a colony of bats all nestled down in the hollow cement blocks. We had laid our suitcases open, so now I had to shake everything out. We gathered the mess and moved to a finished house.

For me, those seemingly little things are the most challenging times to keep cool and win the battle. You reason over the big battles, discuss them, figure them out and then make a decision; but the little ones just happen. There they are, so what to do? They irritate because there is no obvious decision—they are just there in front of you.

We were in the mountains of the Congo, and as we drove up to the top for the service the truck kept conking out. We got to the meeting, had a great time, and they fed us and were so gracious. We slept in the truck. That was an experience in itself, but we had planned for it, so we were ready. We finally found a mechanic and discovered the problem was the carburetor. None were available, so they rigged up a jerry can of fuel sitting outside the passenger window, with the window washer tube leading from the jerry can to the carburetor, so we could get back down the mountain and buy a new one.

My job was to hold the jerry can steady outside my window, as the roads were rocky and we had some rivers to pass through. We made it down the mountain and onto the flat, and then our invention gave up. So up came the hood, and soon every man and child was peering into the engine.

Something Lew had eaten was disagreeing with him, so he came to me wanting TP.

I asked, "Where are you going to go?"

Pointing across the field he said, "There is an outhouse over there."

Off he went like the pied piper with a troop of kids following him. He told me later that when he got to the outhouse, the door was just a sack that only covered the top half of the door space.

I asked, "What did you do about the kids?"

"Nothing. I guess they just wanted to see if I was white all over!"

We had to send to Burundi for the carburetor, so we stayed a few more nights in the truck. Life in Africa!

Then there are the hard battles, which seemed to come when I least expected them. They were big, but they left us with a renewed confidence that He that is in us is stronger that He that is in the world.

Spiritual Battles

> "We wrestle not against flesh and blood,
> but against principalities, against powers,
> against the rulers of the darkness of this world,
> against spiritual wickedness in high places."
> —Ephesians 6:12

While living in Uganda, we went through a period of demonic attacks on Lew. Once I woke up in the middle of the night and there was a big hole in the wall, with grotesque faces grinning through the wall laughing at Lew, who was sound asleep. I sat up and began to command them to go. He was God's man, and they had no right to him!

Another time I saw a large net fall from the ceiling and try to gather Lew up while he was sound asleep. I called out, "I will help you!" and sat up. By this time Lew was awake, and as I told him what I saw, we began to pray in the spirit, knowing that the enemy didn't know what we were praying. The atmosphere cleared and we slept peacefully.

On one of our trips into Zaire, we were staying with missionaries. I awoke as a large snake began to curl itself around Lew. I knew it was a python. "Stop it!" I cried, which of course woke Lew up, and together we cursed the snake and cast it away from the room. We wondered at such a pattern.

On our next trip back to Portland, the Lord to spoke to Lew through a young prophet that Lew had trained up in Vancouver: "The enemy will try to destroy you, but will not accomplish it. Stand firm, do my work and I will keep you." Lew had a heart attack in the next season back in Uganda, which weakened his heart, but it continued beating until at 80 years of age his heart failed. It had done its job until Lew fulfilled all that God had called him to do. Thank you, Jesus, for your grace and love.

Recover All

David had been chased all over the country by King Saul and his army. Why? Because David was a threat to Saul. The prophet Samuel had anointed David King in place of Saul, because of Saul's disobedience to God's commands. David had a couple of opportunities to kill Saul, but couldn't, because Saul was God's anointed king, and David believed in God's purposes (1 Samuel 27:1).

David and his men moved to Ziklag with King Achish in Gath, which was Goliath's home country. David had won Israel's battle over the Philistines years before when he killed Goliath, and now he was living in Golitha's territory. Now, Saul stopped bothering him and David became one of the King's chief guardians in Ziklag. He and his men lived there a year and four months.

As time went by, David was busy doing his skirmishes to protect Israel at night, fooling Achish all the time, and trying to make himself feel better about where he was—in Gath, Philistine country, Israel's enemy.

The time of accountability came, and Israel's enemies went to war against them. David and his men were included in the army of Israel's enemy. They lived there, ate there, loved there, and sang there, so to all intents and purposes they had become one of them, doing what they did while in Israel's eyes deceiving the enemy. David was noncommittal. His conviction and passion were buried, and discouragement had clouded his purpose. (See 1 Samuel 28:2.)

David, what about your call, your anointing, your destiny: kingship in Israel? Are you going to spend your future in Gath? What about those following you? They came to you in debt, discouraged, distressed and discontent. They have followed you and fought with you faithfully, and now what? However, God had not lost sight of David.

Achish's allies recognized David.

The enemy knows who I am. He watches me. He knows what I can do and what I have done. I am of no value to him, only to God, because He has called me and anointed me to do exploits. My flesh may be weak, but the devil knows me and my authority with my God! I don't need to run in discouragement. God is with me, and I am valuable no matter what. Do I really believe that? (See 1 Samuel 29:1–5)

David had defected from Israel. He had done a good job of secretly maintaining a position in Israel, but was living in the country of Gath. He had become a deceiver, which is sin. Being lukewarm and on the fence is very dangerous. Poor David. I wonder what plans he was making in his mind. What a predicament. Rejected again, but this time by the enemy. It was time to take a good look at what had occurred. His losing sight of God's promise and allowing discouragement and weariness of battle against the un-anointed flesh of Saul had caused him to open the door to war with other enemies of Gath, which included his own people, Israel. He had actually become part of the enemy that was against God's people. What a mess he had created!

David argued with Achish, and assured him that he and his men would be okay to continue in the battle. Was his plan to deceive Achish again and allow his own people Israel to be killed? Achish apologized and sent David and his men back home to Ziklag. (See 1 Samuel 29:6–11.)

Talk about distress. While the men were off to war, a common enemy of the Philistines and Israelites, the Amalekites, raided Ziklag and took everything. Time to justify yourself for your actions, David. Saul is after your life. Achish and his friends have rejected you. Your wife, children and possessions are gone. Everything is destroyed. Your mighty men have lost everything and are ready to stone you. They just can't understand!

What have I done? What is the matter with me? I have cut myself off from my people and joined the enemy's camp, because the unanointed flesh (Saul) is after me, when God has anointed me to be *King. What was I thinking?*

David strengthened himself in the Lord. Remember the shepherd boy in the fields, watching the sheep? Remember him killing a lion and a bear? Remember the battle against Goliath? Remember . . .

"Saul has slain his thousands and David his ten thousands."
(See 1 Samuel 30:1–7)

David called for the ephod. "I need to hear the voice of God. Let me prepare myself to hear the voice of God. Forgive me, Lord, I am here again, ready to do whatever you say. I am so sorry. Cleanse me. I humble myself in your presence. What shall I do? I am listening. God spoke.

"In the day that I cried out, You answered me,
and made me bold with strength in my soul."
—Psalm 138:3

"Pursue, overtake, recover all."
—1 Samuel 30:8

Who is willing to go and fight? 600 men ran as far as the brook Besor, then 200 of the men said, "We will stay here. We are too weary to go on. We will guard the supplies and wait here until you return." 400 men went on with David.

Together they did exactly as the Lord said to do:

- Pursued: requires effort, ingenuity, purpose, strategy, action
- Overcame: requires persistence. They didn't stop and they pasted the enemy.
- Recovered all: plus more!

The attitude of Gath had rubbed off on some of David's men. They looked at the 200 men who were weary and didn't help recover all and said, they didn't deserve the spoil that was collected. But David had learned his lesson. No, he said:

"But as his part is who goes down to the battle, so shall his part be who stays by the supplies, they shall share alike."
—1 Samuel 30:24

David even sent some of the spoil home to Judah and his friends to say, "See how the Lord has delivered me, I am ready to fulfill my mission!" (1 Samuel 30:26).

Saul the un-anointed flesh, his three sons, his armor bearer, and all his men died together in the very battle that David was rescued from. David became King and went on to fulfill his destiny (1 Samuel 31:6).

What an example that account is to me. No matter what happens, or what others think, Almighty God is in control. He has a timetable, and if I will trust Him and follow Him, His destiny for me will be fulfilled in His way and timing. I don't need to defend myself, just trust and follow Him into my destiny.

Home Again

When we returned home permanently from Uganda we settled in Portland, Oregon for a season. We bought a condo, then sold it to purchase a little house that we sold seven years later. We then moved to Chehalis/Centralia to be part of a small church there. We did well with the sale of our Oregon house, so invested all our profit and inheritance in our dream home. The down payment into the mortgage was substantial, and the payments were doable. It was a lovely, simple home, just exactly what we wanted in property size and square footage, and my love for beautiful décor. We put together a beautiful yard of flowers, and we were set! We loved it. This was it. We were retired!

Then came the recession. Our income declined. At first I went to work, then Lew could not be left alone, and I had to look after him, so in the end we could not sustain the mortgage payments and had to declare bankruptcy. It was the hardest thing I had ever faced up to that day! So many questions. Why, God? I don't understand. But it was done, and we moved on.

It is over now. The required years have passed, I am in Canada, Lew is in heaven, and life goes on. As my years go by I realize that with each battle, I must pursue my destiny, overtake the enemy, and recover all that I may have lost in the process. I cannot live in the past. It is done. I can only move on, trusting in Him. His word never fails. He does not change. After all, He is the Almighty God and He has His Banner over me for all my days.

I had the privilege of going on a Missions Trip to India with some ladies from City Bible Church, in Portland Oregon. We had a great time. I enjoyed the fellowship with the ladies, as well as the ministry opportunity. India needs Jesus! I felt such a depression while there. The lack of laughter and joy—the heaviness—was hard for me. The team was wonderful, ready to serve and do whatever their hand found to do. I don't remember all the places we went. It seems we arrived in New Deli and then went south. It was so humid and hot. My roommate Paula and I despaired of the heat. We couldn't get cool enough. We would go into our room, strip, and beg the air conditioners to cool us down.

The ministry was wonderful, and everyone just cooperated with the whole. There were four of us who preached, and I was one, so I had my opportunity and as always I enjoyed ministering. I particularly enjoyed praying for the ladies we were ministering to. The battle was not easy, but the Lord helped us. Usually when I go into a new culture, I seek to be ministered to also, and the Lord met me there in a very special way.

At one point we traveled by train. We had bought material and had Indian dresses made for us all, so this one time we were standing on the train platform, waiting for the trains. Someone said we looked like the teapot in the movie "Beauty and the Beast"! We laughed and started to sing, "I'm a little teapot short and stout, here is my handle and here is my spout. When I get all warmed up then I shout, "Tip me over and pour me out," with all the actions of pouring our tea out! I'm sure whoever saw us thought these white lady evangelists had lost their minds. But for us, we laughed and laughed, and it was an opportunity to release some of the pressure of the principalities and powers that can rob one's joy.

I preached in a sari. Now that is an accomplishment. With all that material wrapped around me and over my head to keep it covered, I was hot, and sweating like a garden watering can. But the Lord was with me. I could sense His presence, and the response was overwhelming. I was thankful for the opportunity to be ministering there.

A mighty fortress is our God, A bulwark never failing;
Our helper He, amid the flood Of mortal ills prevailing.
For still our ancient foe Doth seek to work us woe;His
craft and pow'r are great, And, armed with cruel hate,
On earth is not his equal.

Did we in our own strength confide,
Our striving would be losing.
Were not the right Man on our side,
The Man of God's own choosing:
Dost ask who that may be? Christ Jesus, it is He;
Lord Sabaoth His Name, From age to age the same,
And He must win the battle.

—Martin Luther

Left: Marion and Lew at Glad Tidings Youth Camp

Above, Left and Below: Glad Tidings Youth Camp

Left and Below:
Youth Camp
Campfire

Left and Below:
Pacific National
Exhibition,
One Way Inn
Outreach

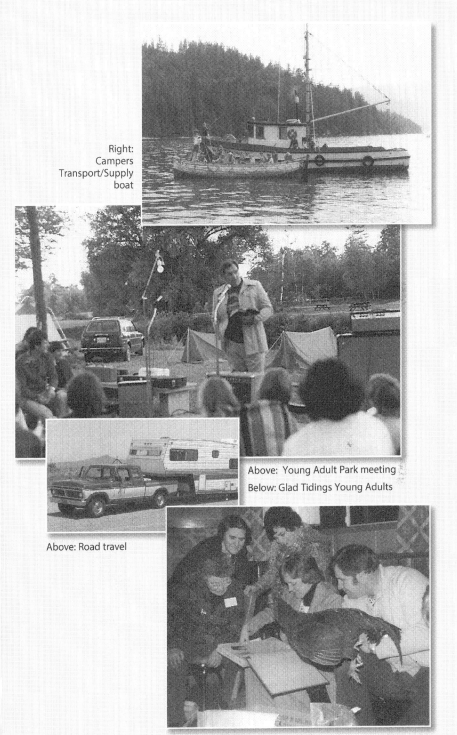

Right:
Campers
Transport/Supply
boat

Above: Young Adult Park meeting

Below: Glad Tidings Young Adults

Above: Road travel

CHAPTER SEVEN

Mr. MERCY!

P rayer and Praise are the keys that unlock the doors!"
Somehow I know the right key for the next door will
be provided to open that door ahead of me. I have
learned that whatever the season of life I am in, whatever the trials,
whatever the joys, as I ask, seek and knock He hears and the key
works. The door opens, I walk through, and my being rises in praise,
understanding what He is able to do for me. That amazing balance of
prayer and praise causes me to fly into his perfect will.

Pray with thanksgiving, pray fervently, pray with understanding,
pray in the Spirit, pray always, pray continually. It brings healing to
the soul.

Whisper a prayer in the morning,
whisper a prayer at noon,
Whisper a prayer in the evening to
keep your heart in tune.

~   ~   ~

Praise Him, praise Him.
Praise Him in the morning, praise Him in the noon time.
Praise Him, praise Him,
Praise Him when the sun goes down.

In my youth I was taught the importance of prayer and praise, the two wings that throughout my life would carry me through every storm and every circumstance. With both my wings—prayer and praise—I have the power to fly into my destiny. In those days our church had a large prayer room open daily for anyone to use at any time. In that prayer room I learned to use the Prayer Key to direct my life, to guide the missionaries, to heal the sick, and to encourage the weary. Then, combining the prayer with praise, I experienced full confidence that when the lock was released the door would swing open and I would see the flight clear before me. It went something like this: prayer one hour before the service, prayer during the service, and prayer after the service, combined with my other wing, Praise.

Out of that I discovered that prayer was an attitude of the heart. I could actually be praying always, watching and seeing my prayer key open many doors during the day without even being conscious of praying, and then hearing myself say, "I praise you, Jesus, for a safe flight."

"The prayer of faith will save the sick,
and the Lord will raise him up.
And if he has committed sins, he will be forgiven.
Confess your trespasses to one another,
And pray for one another, that you may be healed.
The effective, fervent prayer of a righteous man avails much."
—James 5:15, 16

In this chapter I have chosen to say thank you to many of my friends that have been with me through the years in so many different circumstances, in so many different places around the world. I know they have known when to pray for me. I have felt their prayers in the hard times, and their friendship has warmed my heart.

Sweet hour of prayer! Sweet hour of prayer:
That calls me from a world of care,
And bids me at my Father's throne
Make all my wants and wishes known:
In seasons of distress and grief,
My soul has often found relief;
And oft escaped the temper's snare
By thy return, sweet hour of prayer!
—William Bradbury (1859)

Thank you for your great faith, your love, your hope in Him, and your trust in me when you cry for mercy 'cause I pulled a boo-boo!

I have gone through my pictures, and with each one a memory has come to mind, and I thank my Lord for our times together. Some have strengthened me with words of encouragement, some with a sermon, some with a quick text, a card or an email, and some just being there with a hug when comfort was all I needed. Others have said, "I don't feel good about that. Let's pray some more." "He will guide you. Here's a suggestion."

I appreciate you all so much. I know I will miss remembering some on the journey, but I am going to take that chance, because I feel I need to say, "Thank you."

Mr. "MERCY"!

Conrad was one of those men that I admired so much. I met him when he and his family came to Glad Tidings, and he fell in love with the praise and worship. Shortly after his wife became ill with cancer and passed away quickly. They had three children, and it was very difficult for all of them. Time when by, and on a Tuesday evening after the service he came looking for me:

"Well, who do you have picked for me, Marion?"

I was taken back, thought a moment, and suggested one off the top of my head.

He said, "Mercy, no. That wouldn't work for me."

I laughed, and said, "How 'bout Marie?"

"Marie Callahan?" he answered with a surprised look. "Never, because she is fully committed to Maureen."

I replied, "Well, she can always say no. It won't hurt to ask!"

He walked away, and I didn't know that he had gone straight upstairs where she was working in the office to ask for a date. That was 38 years ago, and now history, as she obviously said, "Yes!"

Conrad and Marie

Conrad and Marie became special friends to us. While we lived in the states and Uganda, their home was our Bed and Breakfast when we made our trips home to the Vancouver area. They encouraged us and helped us through our tough times. They both were full of great faith, counseling us when we didn't know which way to turn. Thank you Marie. You are a faithful friend.

Bill and Evelyn

Bill and Evelyn were always near to us, although we were separated by miles. Our calling and development in ministry were similar, yet far apart in actuality. As a teen I met Evelyn at camp. Her pastor was Bill. She married Bill, and they came to camp together. We became best friends, I think because our goals were the same. His strength in ministry was prophetic, and his goal was to establish a college to train young people for ministry, especially in the prophetic realm. Lew's strength was as a pastor, and his goal was to do the same, only in Africa, where we established a training Institute to train pastors and teach them to be self supporting. When we came home and were together, it was like we had never been apart. They were very special people in our lives. Evelyn passed away five years ago, and Bill is travelling continuously, ministering around the world in the churches led by pastors who were trained in Christian International School of Theology. Bill, thank you so much for your friendship.

Howard and Donna

What a great, solid couple they are. From the time they were courting as teenagers God's hand has guided them. They have been faithful servants through the years and have honored Him in all things. Howard's success in the music field has been directed by the Holy Spirit. He developed CCLI, and then most recently was recognized in the Music Hall of Fame. I appreciate you both so much. I thank you with a grateful heart.

Terry and Susan, my dear friends.

I met Susan years ago in Tennessee, and then Terry later in Pasadena, California. Their love for worship was our common bond, and then we connected very deeply over our love for missions. Every time we were back on this side of the water they invited us to visit. We would talk for days as they gave us solid counsel. Thank you for your open home and counsel.

Lawrence and Iris

I would love to live near our friends in the North, except for the cold and deep, deep snow. They pastor a great church, very international and exciting. They have always made me feel very much at home. I was with them twice this year. First, besides preaching we walked on water—frozen Lake Louise. We actually rode in a sleigh on the lake pulled by two huge horses. Then later, I was in Edmonton again to attend Gerda's memorial service and stayed with them over the weekend. What a great time we had together. Thank you for your great hospitality and love.

Hugh and Audrey

Hugh and Audrey were the founders of the Full Gospel in Uganda. With the call to Africa and the full support of Glad Tidings, they pioneered the gospel in a country that had never had a resident missionary or pastor proclaim the Gospel of the Kingdom and see the results of His power. The message spread throughout the region and over the walls, where now there are thousands of believers in churches proclaiming God's great grace. By the way, Hugh, my only brother, is my hero. Thank you, Hugh and Audrey.

Derrill and Michal

My Pastor. We came home from Uganda permanently the same year that they pioneered Life Center in Centralia. After popping in and out of Life Center for nine years, we decided to move and lived there for nine more years. We loved the church. The people were the best. Derrill began my journey with me when Lew was diagnosed. Next to my Pastor Lew, he ran a close second. We built our dream home, enjoyed a good flood, and I learned to work in the commercial world. Quite a lesson! Thank you for many Sundays of good preaching! Lew told him so many times: "I wish I had said that!"

> *Sweet Hour of prayer, sweet hour of prayer,*
> *Thy wings shall my petition bear.*
> *To Him whose truth and faithfulness*
> *Engage the waiting soul to bless.*
> *And since He bids me seek His face,*
> *Believe His word, and trust His grace,*
> *I'll cast on Him my every care*
> *And wait for thee, sweet hour of prayer!*
> *—William Bradbury (1859)*

Lyle & Lu

Lyle & Lu were our neighbors in Still Waters Estate. When Lew needed to live in a better security situation, we moved into a very nice apartment in a senior living community in Centralia, Washington. In our lives, Lyle went back many years. Lu was part of the Bradley family that we have known since the days of Crescent Beach camp. Lyle was Pastor in Tieton, Washington, where we visited to minster years ago. We have the same roots as far as the revival goes, so it was a great blessing to be in the same community. We walked together, prayed together, and just enjoyed fun with a cup of tea (Marion) and coffee (Lew). They were good, loving neighbors. Thank you for loving us.

Jim and Barb

Jim and Barb were our missionary friends in Nairobi. Their place was a haven for us when the wars were happening in Uganda. We would arrive at their place done in and ready for peace, and the coffee was on and the bed was made. We spent our days grocery shopping and got our first Alsatian German Shepherd watchdogs from them. We talked for hours, and prayed together as they comforted us and encouraged us to keep on going on. We ministered in their Bible School and enjoyed their fellowship so much. Thank you—you guys are the best.

Jonathan and Kristi

They were with Derrill and Michal from the beginning of pioneering Life Center. Jonathan became the Pastor when Derrill went to Portland to be with Pastor Frank. Jonathan was a very successful business man. We weren't sure he would make the change, but he did, and because he had been with the church from its beginning, the transition was comfortable for us, as we continued to flow together for the good of the town. It wasn't long after the transition that we moved back to Canada to have extended care for Lew. I have remained close to them and still feel like I belong to Centralia.

Daniel and Nan

They have kept in touch with us, and came to Chilliwack to help me celebrate my 80th birthday, and represented my "Thank You" to the many friends God gave us in Centralia Life Center. How much we enjoyed our resident years with them. Lew especially enjoyed their country home in Mossy Rock, as we enjoyed their hospitality many times. We had a common love for dogs, so our dogs were friends also!

Lew's Davids

Thank you for the friendship with Lew. I don't know how it came about that his closest friends were Davids. I know most were coming for his 80th birthday celebration, but he had his third ambulance ride that weekend and ended up staying in the hospital for observation over the weekend. Thank you for planning to come. We were all very disappointed. Mari Lou and family were here for the weekend, and we spent his birthday celebrating in the nurse's lounge. Thank you for attending Lew's celebration service. All were there except Dave Brace, who came home from Africa only to go into the hospital himself, and as well David Burns, who was in New Zealand. Lew loved you . . . Dave and Vi; Dave and Velma; Dave and Anne; Dave and Karen, Dave and Fran; Dave and Audra and Dave and Ethel.

"Just as lotions and fragrance give delight,
a sweet friendship refreshes the soul."
"You use steel to sharpen steel,
and one friend sharpens another."
—Proverbs 27:9; 27:17

Old Friends Good Food (OFGF)

What a blessing they all have been to me since we moved back to Canada. They met us with a big party, celebrated our return, and gave us a car with the maintenance provided for a year. I have so enjoyed becoming reacquainted with our longtime friends. This September it will be four years since we crossed the border to live in our homeland once again.

Joseph and Winnie

Our son in Uganda. Joseph came to us having just finished college, and ready to be trained for ministry. His family had been separated by the wars, and he ran for his life. He ended up in Kampala, took shelter with one of the mothers in our church, and she helped him finish his education. He married Winnie, and they have four young adult children. Joseph is still one of the Pastors in Life Church, and has weathered all the storms with his prophetic spirit, ministering to the pastors and congregation alike.

Thank you to all our friends in the various places where we ministered. I can't remember all of the places we went after we left Glad Tidings, Vancouver and crossed to the USA. Then there was the Christian International circuit we made in the eastern USA—

such great churches, and we made wonderful new friends. I thank you all for accepting and loving us.

I have discovered that to be a prayer and praise person, it takes great faith, because I don't always want to do it. Jesus placed high importance on faith. The word commands us to praise Him whether we want to or not, and to pray without ceasing. Faith's greatest enemy is worry. Worry produces fear. Fear and faith cannot mix; they are like oil and water. They just don't mix! Jesus said, "Have faith in God," and let Him take care of the problem His way.

In this crazy, confusing and angry world of ours, we cannot let fear overtake us. Our faith must be that God is in control. Then when we pray, we believe. Our faith kicks in and we begin to praise Him for the answer. What answer He gives is not our issue. We just have faith, believe and pray.

I am so thankful for all those who prayed in faith for us through all these years, when fear could have overtaken us. So many times we needed a victory immediately, and as we cried out to the Lord He heard the prayers of His people on our behalf, even when we didn't have the space or energy to pray. I can't possible begin to mention everyone, but here are a few. We have been abundantly blessed and I thank you for your faithfulness.

So many more, such a vast multitude—we will meet you all around the throne. Many friends allowed God to use them to be instruments of His Mercy, as they prayed and believed, sometimes not knowing what or why they were praying.

My only sister, Ruth, I thank her for being such a faithful friend. She ministered with us for so many years. We counted on her, and she never failed to accomplish her task. What a woman of God she was. I learned faithfulness from her example. We dubbed Ruth with the second name, "Faithful."

Lew's brother Bob accepted Lew's call to ministry, which required him to leave the family business. Then he supported us in our desire to be in Africa. He encouraged us when we left for Uganda the first time, and Lew appreciated how he looked after their parents in his absence. He had such a big heart. When we returned home after the second time in Uganda, he even tried to teach us how to play golf. It wasn't particularly successful, but we had fun trying! All our parents, and Ruth and Bob are all in Heaven now, and Lew is with them now, as they wait for the rest of us.

Encamped along the hills of light,
Ye Christian soldiers rise,
And press the battle 'ere the night
Shall veil the glowing skies.
Against the foe in vales below
Let all our strength be hurled.
Faith is the victory, we know,
That overcomes the world.

His banner over us is love,
Our sword the Word of God.
We tread the road the saints above
With shouts of triumph trod.
By faith, they like a whirlwind's breath,
Swept on o'er every field;
The faith by which they conquered death
Is still our shining shield.
Faith is the victory,
Oh glorious victory that overcomes the world.
—Ira D. Sankey

I remember a time in my life when my world turned upside down. I was in deep, stormy waters and I couldn't breath. We were in a new pastorate, and the leadership was not familiar with me, or our message, or the team ministry that Lew and I were called to flow in. As a result, there arose conflict, misunderstandings and criticism. This resulted in my deep discouragement, even to questioning the call and destiny of God for my life. I wanted to quit. Lew recognized the desperation of the situation and immediately sent me to spend time with a "father in the faith" and his wife, David Schoch and Audene.

I spent hours in prayer with them, searching the Word to find afresh what God had to say about His purpose for me. Then more hours, walking miles on the beach, listening to the waves rolling in on the sand, crying, yelling, groaning, and falling on my knees, begging God to release me from the captivity of "the ministry." My faith was low, but I prayed through. He had compassion on me and His mercy took over. I made it through 30 more years of fulltime ministry.

> In your POVERTY, He is WEALTH
> In your FOOLISHNESS, He is WISDOM
> In your PAIN, He is your HEALER
> In your DOUBT, He is your FAITH
> In your DISCOURAGEMENT, He is your ENCOURAGER
> In your FAILURE, He is your SUCCESS
> In your WEAKNESS, He is your STRENGTH
> In your LONLINESS, He is your FRIEND
> In your WANT, He is your SUPPLY
> In your CAPTIVITY, He is your DELIVERER
> In your DARKEST HOUR, He is your LIGHT

"Indeed, we count them blessed who endure.
You have heard of the perseverance of Job
And seen the end intended by the Lord—
That the Lord is very compassionate and merciful."
—James 5:11

He will never fail you. Run to Him . . . *Call* upon Him . . . Take hope in Him. His mercy and love surround you.

Listen to Lew telling about one of the times he had to reach out for God's mercy when in a tight situation. "I had been on 'safari' holding meetings with pastors in a number of village churches and was extremely tired upon arriving home. So I took time to rest for a few hours. I was awakened by Marion and saw soldiers in the room, one with an AK-47 pointed at her, and the first words I recognized were, "We are going to kill this woman." Marion is standing there, carefully hiding our jewelry down her skirt, as well as the keys to our vehicles, as calmly as if this was an everyday occurrence."

"Why?" You got it. The Lord is our keeper. His mercy is new every day. It took me what seemed an eternity to catch my breath and begin breathing again. Obviously, my first response was fear. Then the Lord with his compassion and mercy came on the scene and a Holy Ghost boldness fell on me, obviously the same one that was on Marion, and I sat up, stood up, and began to take control of the situation.

"How?" "Why?" Yes sir, He was there, and He is our only hope, and I knew Marion was praying hard! The word says, "He shall preserve you from all evil." Yes, even from AK-47s, even from soldiers, thieves, sickness and fear. It must have been quite a sight to see two soldiers with their guns pointed at us, walking down the hallway as we claimed the Lord was with us, and they had better leave our home, or we would not be held responsible for what would happen to them.

"When they went outside the house, our house help heard them saying, 'We cannot go back into the house. The white man has a secret weapon, and we do not know what he will do to us.' Our response was to fall on our knees and give thanks to the Lord for honoring His word on our behalf. We can say the Lord poured His mercy on us big time!"

> "Through the Lord's mercies we are not consumed,
> Because His compassions fail not.
> They are new every morning; Great is your faithfulness.
> "The Lord is my portion," says my soul, t
> herefore I hope in Him!"
> —Lamentations 3:22–24

There are three words we use when thinking of mercy: pity, sympathy or compassion. They mean literally suffering with another, hence having pity or sympathy for another. Compassion includes pity and sympathy, with strong emotion that demands action and mercy. The action can be feeling for someone as the result of any kind of experience in life.

- Because of Israel's disobedience they received in no pity from God. (Isaiah 63:7–9)
- This time God was full of compassion and forgave Israel. (Psalm 78:38, 39)
- Jesus healed the lepers. (Mark 1:41)
- Jesus healed the blind men. (Matthew 20:34)
- Jesus raised the lady's son from the dead. (Luke 7:13)
- The father of the Prodigal Son. (Luke 15:20)
- Jesus prayed for harvest labourers, and was moved with compassion for the people. (Matthew 9:36)

Peter addresses the church,

"Finally all of you be of one mind,
having compassion for one another;
love as brothers, be tenderhearted, be courteous;
not returning evil for evil or reviling for reviling,
but on the contrary blessing,
knowing that you are called to this,
that you may inherit a blessing."
—1 Peter 3:8, 9

Compassion

Our close friend Conrad (whom I call Mr. Mercy) and his wife were given the ministry of Mercy. They lived to serve others. "Mercy" became the expression of his heart. Their lovely home was open to anyone who needed help, counsel, food, a bed, a home, and even a party—just anything. I remember Conrad gathering young men off the street; actually, he chased a young that came into and left his jewelry store, because Conrad felt he needed Jesus. He nurtured him, and the young man came to Jesus. Later he married and is now a grandfather, still serving Jesus. Conrad is in heaven, enjoying the fruit of his love for the young men who needed Jesus. One of these men, a heron addict, was found in the church men's room passed out. Help came, he found Jesus, and Conrad, moved with compassion, became his friend and nurtured him into ministry. He married, has a family, and served the Lord all the days of his life. Mercy!

Conrad and Marie took in folk from other countries that needed help and a home. One of them came with a young son who had a pet rabbit. When we came to stay with them, there was this cage with a rabbit in her beautiful kitchen. I was stunned. Would I do that, even in Uganda? When one of the missionaries fell sick with cancer, they opened up their home. Conrad gave up his bed on the main floor so that Marie could look after her 24/7. Marie would have to call the pastor for help whenever the patient fell, because, even together they could not lift her. When she passed, they looked after all her affairs, organizing church folks to sort, sell and give away her things. Mercy!

They hosted many a gathering, serving with joy. Conrad would sit down and play his grand piano as the group worshiped and praised the Lord. Marie is a good cook, and for our 50th anniversary they hosted a reunion of our Glad Tidings youth years with a pie desert bash! Everyone was there. What fun we had remembering—and eating pie! These were my examples of servants full of mercy!

> "The Lord takes pleasure in those who fear Him,
> in those who hope in His mercy.
> —Psalm 147:11

What makes mercy, faith, hope, and trust happen? Love is the ingredient that makes it all work. He loved us, before we loved Him. God is love, so He created His love in us, and then we have the choice to use it to love Him back. The result? As God loved the world and gave, so we love our world and give our love, our mercy, our hope, our faith and our trust so that they can experience His love that is already created in them. Really all they have to do is respond to it. That love is already in us. We just have to let it flow out.

> "Now faith is the substance of things hoped for,
> the evidence of things not seen."
> —Hebrews 11:1

Hope

Hope comes first, then the substance: Faith.

Hope is "Favorable and confident expectation," and, "The happy anticipation of good."

Hope is trusting in something stronger and greater than our own selves for our needs.

Hope is future. Faith is present. Hope in God!

- A Good Hope (Thessalonians 2:16)
- A Blessed Hope (Titus 2:13)
- A Living Hope (1 Peter 1:3)
- A Better Hope (Hebrews 7:19)

> "Why are you cast down O my soul?
> And why are you disquieted within me?
> Hope in God;
> For I shall yet praise Him,
> The help of my countenance."
> —Psalm 42:5

Paradigm

We humans have a tendency in our life journey to give into paradigms. A paradigm is a mindset that blocks one from moving on in life and fulfilling all that God has in their destiny. It will oppress the level of hope in life, if you do not have the whole picture of your future. It will also reduce hope, by obscuring our vision of our future in God and the potential of what God has for us. A paradigm lodged in our minds is a mindset, that limits us. As years pass, the vision is delayed, circumstances hinder us, and the vision is lost.

An example is Abraham & Sarah (Genesis 15:1-6).

Abraham said to the Lord, "I go childless, and the heir of my house is Eliezer of Damascus."

God assured him, "This one shall not be your heir, but one who will come from your own body shall be your heir." Then God brought Abraham outside and said, "Look now towards the heavens. Count the stars, if you are able to number them. So shall your descendants be."

They produced Ishmael, who was another paradigm, another roadblock, another stronghold against the hope in God's promise for a heir.

Finally Isaac was born and later was saved by God from being the sacrificial lamb. The paradigm was broken, the mindset cleared. Abraham now was confident. He had "hooked" onto his hope, and now his faith was alive.

> " Therefore from one man, and him as good as dead,
> were born as many as the stars of the sky in multitude,
> innumerable as the sand that is by the sea shore."
> —Hebrews 11:12

He stopped managing God, and the reward was that his faith grew, and he acted upon and received the promise.

I fell into a paradigm situation when Lew died. I was sure that I was done also. The memory tears flowed, the pity parties came in abundance. I was lost and just sure that it was over. How could I go on without him? What would I do? The waves of grief would not stop. I was alone, and I didn't like it.

Gini Smith sent me her booklet *Jesus Wept and So Did I*. I read it over and over, and one of the chapters was based on the man at the pool of Bethesda. Jesus asked him, "Do you want to be made well?" (see John 5:1–8).

"Yes, Lord. I do. Please help me." He made excuses about why he had been sick and waiting for 38 years. Was I making excuses for staying in my despair? Am I stuck in self-pity? Where are you, Lord? Please speak to me!

The process for the man's healing was, "Get up, Pick up, and Walk." I will never forget the answer. Get up, pick up the dirty self pity mats, and walk, one step at a time. The Spirit said, "I called you when you were a child, and I have not changed my mind."

The phone rang and there came a prophetic word: "Go back to Uganda, Marion, and see what the Lord has done. Rejoice in what has happened upon the foundation you and Lew laid."

I did that, and my life came back together. I was renewed amongst the people that are so dear to me, whom I was called to as a child. I had a paradigm to break, and my hope had to be refocused. It will be 2 years next month since Lew went on his journey to heaven. When I think of the many times we began to write this book and it just didn't gel, but this time the thoughts have flowed like a river. Thank you, Gini. Thank you, Bill.

> *My hope is built on nothing less*
> *Than Jesus blood and righteousness;*
> *I dare not trust the sweetest frame,*
> *But wholly lean on Jesus' name.*
> *His oath, His covenant, His blood,*
> *Support me in the whelming flood;*
> *When all around my soul gives way,*
> *He then is all my hope and stay*
> *On Christ the solid Rock I stand;*
> *All other ground is sinking sand.*
> *—Edward Mote (1791–1874)*

Years ago on one of our trips to Alberta, Lew was asked to plaster a church. Lew was a brick mason, not a plasterer, but he had watched it done many times, so he said, "Sure, I'll do it." It was a small town and everyone knew everyone, so soon the whole town knew this stranger was plastering the church, when there were other residents that could be doing it. After about half the job was done, because Lew was not used to that kind of motion, his arms were feeling the strain and a change developed in his right chest muscle. For the remainder of his life, his upper right chest muscle was larger than his left.

One afternoon as he was up on the ladder working, he heard the roar of a motor and the sound of tires on gravel. Suddenly he realized a small pickup truck was coming full speed at him. He jumped from the ladder and dove onto the porch of the church. The truck sped by, crushing the ladder, but Lew was safe. Thank you, Jesus, for your mercy and grace in protecting him. Mercy!

Lew had a similar experience in Cambridge Bay. He had gone out with one of the men on the skidoo for a ride. It was a cold, freezing day, so he dressed warmly with a wool baklava scarf pulled over his head and neck, with only holes for his eyes to see through. By the time they got back the wool was frozen stuck to his neck, and they had to soak it off. Then it wept, like thawing meat, so when he preached, he held a handkerchief over his neck to catch the drippings. When it had finished dripping, the flesh under his chin was black and hanging. He came back to Vancouver like that. As it healed, the black went away, but the flesh was still sagging. For the rest of his life, he had a turkey chin. The loose flesh never went back to normal.

Mercy!

Through it all, we learned not to lose sight of our Hope. He had called us, and we were following Him wherever He took us, to do whatever He wanted to do.

"God willed to make known what are the
riches of the glory of this mystery
among the Gentiles, which is
Christ in you the hope of glory."
—Colossians 1:27

"Who through Him believe in God,
who raised Him from the dead
and gave Him glory so that your faith
and hope might be in God."
"Be not moved away from the hope
of the gospel which you have heard."
—Colossians 1:23

We can hope in Him, because He has compassion and mercy towards us in our circumstances.

However, the enemy is out to rob, kill and destroy my hope. He wants to build strongholds and raise paradigms in my mind to stop his full destiny from being fulfilled in my life.

"I am judged for the hope of the promise
made unto the fathers;"
—Acts 23:6

"Through the Spirit eagerly wait for the
hope of righteousness by faith."
—Galatians 5:5

When we were on our way to Uganda in 1964, Mari Lou turned five as we were crossing the Atlantic. Our ship was anchored in the outer harbor in Dar es Salaam, Tanzania, because there were so many freighter ships ahead of us, waiting to off load. In order to get to the town, we had to get off our ship and into a lifeboat to get to shore. As we were going down the ladder with Mari Lou in Lew's arms, a strong gust of wind blew and moved the ladder, and Mari Lou slipped. By the mercy of God, a crew member was waiting for us in the lifeboat, right there, and he grabbed her as she fell, pulling her into the lifeboat. She was scared, and we were terrified. These were shark-infested waters. Mercy!

> "Rejoice in the hope of the glory of God."
> —Romans 5:2

> "As a helmet . . . the hope of salvation . . . "
> —1 Thessalonians 5:8

> "Just as you were called in one hope of your calling."
> —Ephesians 4:4

A stronghold-paradigm can get us so easily. It can be a fortified place, a care, a bunker of thought, a protected area in my mind, or a collection of thoughts impregnated with hopelessness that causes me to accept something as unchangeable, something that we know is contrary to the will of God. Fear, rejection, anger, lust, or anything that has hopelessness all around it, and when we think about it, can cause us to embrace it in our thought life, even when we know it is not the will of God. When I allow myself to think contrary to the will of God, I lose. Then I become hopeless and begin to compromise in my mind. The evil one is out to cause hopelessness in my mind, until I don't believe that God will deal with it. Fear, rejection, and hopelessness. Strongholds work in hopelessness, but God wants you to remain hopeful.

> "In hope of eternal life, which God
> promised before time began."
> —Titus 1:2

Paradigms can become resident in my mind if I am influenced by the worldview. It is so negative. Embrace it, and it will develop into a stronghold. Purge your mind from fatalism, as that is the world's point of view. Life experiences can lead me into a paradigm that is hopeless. God must be the strength of my life, and my hope, no matter how hard the situation is. I must assess how I will let this experience affect me.

"I wonder if? Speculations cause me to raise my thoughts above God. I must clear my thoughts. He knows everything, and he will remove the block. Recognize it and confess it.

Antidotes:

- Renew my mind through the Word of God.
- Expose strongholds as inadequate.
- Silence the speculator in my mind.
- Take thoughts captive. Ask the thought: "Did you come from God?"
- Bless and encourage others.
- Praise and thank God, and speculations will go away.

"The God of hope fill you with all joy and peace in believing,
that you may abound in hope by
the power of the Holy Spirit."
—Romans 15:13

I can always be renewed in my mind, so that any Paradigm that sneaks in can be blasted away, when by faith I declare my hope is in God alone. His mercy and His grace will renew my hope and trust, so I can reach out to the world around me. I want them to see what a wonderful thing it is to be a living disciple of Jesus Christ.

"For there is hope for a tree if it is cut down,
That it will sprout again,
And that its tender shoots will not cease.
Though its root may grow old in the earth,
And its stump may die on the ground,
Yet at the scent of water it will bud
And bring forth branches like a plant."
—Job 14:7–9

When the presence of the Lord comes down, it is like rain on a parched ground, and a dried root that seems to have no life comes alive again. I saw it happen in Uganda this year. I am alive! Sometimes I feel cut off, but there is hope. I can enter into His presence by praising Him, and the refreshing will come. When my hope is in God, my faith comes alive. I am not perfect, but he has compassion on me in my humanity and is merciful towards me.

> *Faith turns the night into the day,*
> *Hope drives the doubts and fears away.*
> *And my heart is singing,*
> *With the joy bells ringing.*
> *List' to the pealing of the chimes,*
> *Faith brings the victory every time.*
> *Hallelujah, what a Savior,*
> *And just to know that He is mine!*

Mercy, Faith and Hope, with Thanksgiving, in the expression of our prayers produces the results we are praying about. I must never give up. I am praying to God, and He is the one who has the answer. Sometimes I don't like the answer, but nevertheless it is the answer. It is His grace that upholds us when His answers are not our decision. He paid the price. He is our redeemer, and we are the recipient. We don't deserve to have Him pay any attention to us. It is His grace.

"Mother, you need to rest." Mari Lou said emphatically over the phone.

"I was in the shower, now I am laying down because I don't feel well." I answered

"Where is Dad?" she asked.

"Out doing some errands before we leave for Lynnwood."

" You sound strange. Your words are not clear, they are slurred." She continued, "Stay lying down, wait for Dad, and tell him to take you to the hospital. I will meet you there."

We were scheduled to do a Seminar at Mercy Seat in Lynnwood, and I had been working around the clock to prepare the Power Point for Lew's teaching on the Cross. I guess I had worn myself out. Lew arrived home and came into the bedroom, and there I was in the bed.

I said, "Hi" and smiled. He said, "Your smile is lop-sided. Do you feel okay?"

I said, "No."

He said, "Your words are slurred; something is not right. I'm taking you to the hospital!"

"What about Lynnwood, and the seminar?"

He said, "Forget the seminar! I will call the Chings. I am looking after you. I love you!"

Quickly I dressed, and he helped me into the car. He drove furiously to the hospital, and yes, I was experiencing a TIA. They admitted me, and he cancelled the seminar and waited for the medication to take effect. Mari Lou was already there. We prayed together, and into the ER I went. After a day they sent me home, and the family gathered around my bed. As we chatted, Brian said, "Grandma I want to pray for you." His faith was obvious. He was just a teen, yet he believed. He led the family in prayer, dismissing the enemy with such strength that I knew the Lord had touched me.

I rested that weekend, and then we remembered that we were scheduled to leave for Romania in a week. I begged the doctor to let me go. He agreed if I would promise not to do any ministering. I promised. We went. In Romania I greeted the church, and the pastors looked after me, and we had a wonderful time. I ended up speaking to a special children's gathering, which I enjoyed—relaxed and slow. We stopped in Hungary for a rest before coming all the way home. Mercy!

So many times, in so many circumstances, God was faithful as I cried out to him—sometimes in desperation, sometimes in planned prayer meetings, sometimes driving my car, sometimes in my daily devotions, and always before teaching or preaching.

> *"Continue earnestly in prayer,*
> *being vigilant in it with thanksgiving."*
> —Colossians 4:2

Life Church in Uganda as a whole is my extended family, but I have some specific family members that go back to 1964, when we first went to Uganda, who are still part of Life Church's congregation. There are several, but one family in particular is the Magala family. We hired Johnny Magala as our house manager, and he stayed with us for all the years we spent in Uganda. He has two children that are now grown, married, and are parents. Johnny's wife passed away when the children were teens, so we lived together on the Institute property, and Lew and I became grandparents to the children. Peterson, Johnny's son, is a fine man. He is ready to fulfill his destiny as God shows him each step. Marion is a good mother and wife, who runs a day school and has a very strong musical gift. She had a struggle spiritually for a while, and when she came to herself and returned, she wrote the following songs, expressing her confidence and love for Jesus, her Redeemer and Lord. Thank God that He forgives and forgets! He has that sea that He throws our sins into and forgets them. Here are the words for the songs that she wrote at that time, expressing her heart and soul.

Come Home

You walked away to do your thing,
Live your life like you didn't care.
Eventually it caught up with you and the pain you felt
you don't know what to do.
Your going in and coming out
All spent and are in need
With a longing that can't be filled
And you don't know where else to turn.

Come home 'cuz there's love waiting for you.
Child I think about you.
I gave up my life so you could have one.
Come home 'cuz there's hope waiting for you.
Child I love you so.
I gave up my all so you could have all.
Come home.

You might be scared how I'd treat
you when you walked away,
But I'm here to let you know
It doesn't change the way I feel.
And all I want for you is for you to find
your way back home,
Into the arms of amazing grace and receive
the eternal gift of life.

I'm here for you forever
My arms are open wide
So receive what I offer
Come home
I will heal and set you free, mend your
broken heart now and forever.
Come home.
—Marion Magala

Don't You Worry

Don't you worry it's gonna be okay
Don't you worry He is with you all the way
Don't you worry it's gonna be okay.

Put your worries before him and he will give
you strength to see you through
If things don't go your way His is right beside you
to give you strength
Call on him don't be afraid
He'll see you through the storm, yes he will it's true
I know the cloud is dark but the sun will shine again.

Dust off sadness.
Get back to the mainstream.
Put your dreams together and move forward.
Nothing can stop you now 'cuz you are stronger.
Away to go before, but you know it, you'er gonna fly

He'll make your burdens lighter
He'll make your days brighter,
He'll make you stronger,
He'll take you higher,
He'll take you higher,
He'll take you higher.
—Marion Magala

Left: Uganda--2007
Below: Project-Staff House

Left: Team 2007
Below: Uganda-Kenya 2008

Left: Marion & Ruth

Left: India Marion Layzell-Peterson
Below: Newberg Oregon

Above: Ladies Conference Prayer,
Marion Layzell-Peterson
Right: Leeds UK 2005
Below: Romania

CHAPTER EIGHT

Uganda

Missions is not an activity. It is the purpose of the Church! It began through God's purpose (see Genesis 1:26–28).

Then God said, "Let Us make man in Our image, according to Our likeness; let them have dominion...over all the earth." So God created man in His own image...male and female He created them. Then God blessed them, and God said to them, "Be fruitful and multiply..."

Through Christ's birth, life, crucifixion and resurrection this became reality. The Old Covenant opened the way, and the New Covenant empowers His saints to finish the work. The Old Covenant focused mainly on one nation: Israel, his chosen people.

In the eternal mind of God was another covenant—the New Covenant, given to bring completion and fulfillment to the Old Covenant. There cannot be fulfillment of an old covenant without the success of the new, and obviously there is not a foundation for the new covenant without the success and fulfillment of the old. Permit me the right to be very strong here. Neither covenant can stand on its own merit. Both covenants are connected to one purpose—the formation of the Kingdom of God to enable the eternal purpose of God to be fulfilled. Thank God for the Old Testament with its types, shadows, pictures and purposes. There are not adequate words to express gratitude to God for His infinite love, grace, mercy, greatness and patience for rebellious mankind. Like sheep, we have gone astray. We have turned everyone to His own way. Think about how terrible it would be if it all ended there. Without a doubt, God would be giving us what we deserved. Thank God, He is not that kind of a God. He is merciful, loving and kind—the God of a second chance.

Calvary, the supreme sacrifice, was already in His mind. His sacrifice was already in his eternal purpose. "I will take care of this. I will pay the price for man's deliberate disobedience. I will provide deliverance, restoration, and eternal life. I will cause the pure, perfect, eternal life of my Son, Jesus the Christ, to take his place."

Jesus was born—a miracle birth. He lived on this earth for thirty-three years.

He was crucified—a miracle death.

He arose from the grave—a miracle resurrection—and ascended back to His Father.

He sent the Holy Spirit—a miracle gift for his followers, enabling them to fulfill their destiny.

He gave the Great Commission—His miracle command: "Go ye into all the world and preach the Gospel to every creature."

He gave His followers accompanying power to produce signs and wonders following them—the miracle church!

He gave the Great Commission: go or send the gospel of truth to every creature—a miracle commission.

> Write the vision, and make it plain on tablets,
> That he may RUN who reads it.
> For the vision is yet for an appointed time;
> But at the end it will speak, and it will not lie,
> Though it tarries, wait for it;
> Because it will surely come,
> It will not tarry.
> —Habakkuk 2:2-3

To begin this chapter I have included an article written by Vernon Ruhati (a Ugandan reporter) that I found in my files. He wrote it for an information piece to give to the new pastors joining Ministers Fellowship East Africa, since we were no longer in Uganda.

Lew and Marion Peterson are the co-founders of LewMar Ministries, a nonprofit organization based in Centralia, but serving others throughout the world, including Canada, Mexico, Romania, India, Ethiopia, Brazil and Uganda. Their ministry's heritage is from a strong local church. They began their ministry training in Glad Tidings Church in Vancouver, B.C., and later received their BTh from Christian International University, Florida. Marion was the P.K. (preacher's kid), and Lew had been in the church from his early childhood. They received their training in their local church through their courting years, with the dream of being missionaries to Africa. They were married in February, 1958, and in the first nine months of their marriage Lew worked full-time in the family construction business in the Vancouver area as a brick mason, and Marion as a Cosmetologist. In December 1958 they were appointed to pastor a small church in Abbotsford, BC. Without realizing it, the circumstances in that first pastorate prepared them for their future living and ministry conditions in third world countries.

This first Pastorate paid them $15.00 (Canadian) a week, whether they needed it or not. Both the living quarters and the auditorium were in a warehouse-type building with a raised floor, and they listened to the "Rat Olympics" underneath that floor. Their only child Mari Lou was born while they lived there, with no shower, no hot water and no kitchen. Finally, Lew brought his brick mason talent to Abbotsford and built the church a building, and the "Petes" moved into the basement apartment. They were both ordained during this season and were on their way to fulfilling their life's dream.

Since then, their dream to be in Africa was first realized in 1964, where Lew supervised village pastors and Marion established a choir and a youth ministry. As little girls, Mari Lou and Irene Lubega became best friends. They learned to pray and play together at the church while we were busy. The Safari work in those days was rather difficult. They slept on dung floors and on and under makeshift grass beds and coverings. One time they woke up smelling smoke and then saw the pastor trying to put out a grass fire. Apparently there were army ants in the outhouse The pastor was trying to burn them out, and in doing so he set everything on fire. Obviously, they had to move to a safer place.

Lew supervised Bunyoro District, and on one very stormy, rainy trip they were called to pray for the pastor's wife in the middle of the night. They hurried out into the community, prayed for her in the dark, and hurried back to Hoima town, where they had pitched their tent in the police yard for safety. The next day the pastor came and said his wife was better, and, did we know that the bridge over the river had been washed out? Somehow we had crossed, and the town was buzzing. They saw where the tracks went into the water and came out, and then in and out again as we went home. We didn't even know it! Oh, the peace of God when you are on Kingdom business.

They returned to Canada in 1968 to assist in Glad Tidings, Vancouver. Through the years their service has taken them to various locations throughout the world, including again Uganda, East Africa, where they founded RUN Ministries (Reaching Unto Nations). After their return to Uganda in 1984 they established a strong local church in Kampala, a fellowship of pastors and their churches in Uganda, along with fellowships in the surrounding East African countries, and a Bible Training Institute for Pastors. The Institute, Staff and Petersons all resided on the 20 acres by the shores of Lake Victoria, a beautiful, relaxing setting for living and studying.

In addition to teaching biblical and leadership principles, the Petersons taught the nationals how to grow and produce "exotic" vegetables, such as broccoli, which were then sold to the tourist hotels. Also the pastors were taught how to raise healthy farm animals to sell, supporting their families and paying education fees for their children. The Petes have returned a few times since retiring, the last was 1958 to celebrate their 50th marriage anniversary and their 50th anniversary of ministry. In those visits they found RUN Ministries alive and well.

Lew and Marion say they left their hearts in Uganda when they "retired" to come home in 1997. They just walked away, turning everything over to the Nationals—their notes, teachings, vehicles, and household items. They didn't even bring a knife or fork home. The ministry has continued to flourish and grow in all aspects.

—Vern

Conference Thank You's

Pastor Martin Odhiambo of Kenya writes:

We must once again thank God for using you to bring the gospel to Uganda in the early years and be able to produce men and women who are truly servants at heart.

This year we started our own Bible school in our church, yet open to all churches in this city. Our outlines are from the books sent to us through you. Pastor Lew, God used you to be a blessing to us and probably these good men of God will never get the chance to see their work here in us, but eternity will reveal to them their good work through these few books that were put in the hands of such needy people.

Vernon Ruhati, Kampala, Uganda writes:

It was great to have you in Uganda. Your love for our country has not stopped at all. May God give you longer life that you may see more fruit of your sons and daughters in Uganda. I, for one, recognize you as our spiritual parents, and you have endured some of us as we were going through it all.

Bishop Felix Ochieng Oriwa of Kenya writes:

I am writing to thank you for having blessed my heart during the conference. I felt married to your vision and felt part and parcel of what you are doing. I undertook to pray for you and I have started to do so. Thank you so much for such a rich background and deep, sound message. Pastor Marion challenged me so much with her teaching on the covenants.

Pastor William Upendo of Sudan writes:

Here I am, finally thrown at the feet of these great men of God. I am so grateful. Your teaching, Pastors Peterson and Marion, have re-ignited me, and I am on fire again for the Lord.

~ ~ ~

Life in Africa is so different. The evening sounds of crickets and frogs, then the early morning sounds of birds chirping, the rumble of thunder over the lake, with the smell of charcoal burning in the valley below, along with the chatter of the workers in the banana plantation next to the hotel, the laughter of the children, and the pounding of the mallet as the women grid the corn and peanuts. The pace is so much slower. Plans are made with good intentions, and then one goes with the flow! Maneuvering in the traffic is indescribable. I found the best way to avoid a stroke was to close my eyes and pretend to be resting. What you can't see won't hurt you!

This trip we spent five days in Kenya accompanied by Pastor Joseph Kibirige. Joe and Nancy Losee had invited us to minister in the Pastor's Conference in Kitale, Kenya. Joe and Nancy are doing a great job travelling from church to church, teaching "Foundations" classes to pastors and congregations that have never had doctrinal foundations taught to them. It was a great time of ministry—such a thirsty and hungry assembly of pastors drinking in the Word like sponges. We were thrilled with Joseph's ministry—such maturity and growth as he ministered prophetically, in counsel and in teaching. The climax of the conference was an awesome communion service where we made covenant with each other, establishing a deep relationship between them and the brothers in Uganda.

We were invited by Glad Tidings Temple to visit Uganda after being gone for 17 years. Uganda had gone through "hell on earth" years under reign of Idi Amin and Milton Obote and was beginning to come out of the devastation of those war (coup) years.

When we arrived in Uganda we were shocked and torn apart by the devastation we saw, both in the land and in the people. As we ministered our hearts were broken, especially for the new generation of college age, who had known nothing but war and devastation their entire lives. We ministered at a Saturday Youth Convention, and as we came into the auditorium the youth were singing, "I will build again the foundations." We wept brokenheartedly. We both heard the Holy Spirit speak to us, "It is time to come back to the land of your calling and rebuild the foundations in establishing the next generation in "present day truth." Most of those who became our leadership team were in that Youth Conference.

> "For it pleased the Father that in Him
> all the fullness should dwell.
> And by Him to reconcile all things to Himself,
> by Him, whether things on earth or things in heaven,
> having made peace through the blood of His cross."
> —Colossians 1:19, 20

March 1984

On the plane going home to the States we began to talk and listen to the Holy Spirit's voice. He led us to Habakkuk 2:2, 3. This scripture became our theme, and from it came the name of our ministry, RUN Ministries (Restore Uganda Now Ministries, later adjusted to Reaching Unto Nations Ministries).

Lew asked, "Well, what do you think?"

"You first." I replied.

"We have to go back and help the Pastors," Lew commented.

"How? When? Money? Who?"

"I promised Joshua we would be back to stay in a year. We won't build a church or a Bible College, but an Institute to help pastors with churches. Our home church will be Makerere Full Gospel Church, and we will be a branch of the Full Gospel Churches of Uganda. We were to "Write the vision, make it plain on tablets, that he may

RUN who reads it." We knew we were to start a training Institute to train pastors to RUN with the vision. We knew we were definitely going back to Uganda. so when we arrived home in Yuba City we began the process of packing up, readying ourselves to minister in association with the Full Gospel Churches."

Plans began to form in our minds. We had a big vision, much too big for us. We had no money, so we just began to pray (lots) and travel (lots), telling the vision to everyone who would listen, including Bible Temple in Portland, Oregon. The vision included:

- Leadership Training Institute – beginning by traveling to outlying pastors and churches
- Self-sustaining Training (agriculture and farming)
- Pastor's Conferences
- Primary Schools

It took us one year to make the transitions. We resigned our ministry in Yuba City, California, married our daughter, buried both my parents, and, while traveling to raise the money for our new adventure had a major car wreck, which resulted in surgery for me.

Then prophet Ernest Gentile spoke: "You go to do one thing. I send you to do another. Through the midst of confusion and ploy for power, I will fulfill my purpose!" What did that mean?

March 1985

We arrived to reside in Uganda to help Gospel Mission. We asked Pastor Joshua if RUN could be recognized and stated in their documents as a ministry of Gospel Mission. He agreed that we would work together and would add RUN Ministries to Gospel Mission documents. RUN would travel, ministering with the established pastors and churches, to encourage and help them be renewed in what God was saying in the church worldwide today. RUN had no desire to start a church or a Bible School for "would-be" pastors. We desired to work with our original mission that we had been with since the beginning in 1960.

RUN's container arrived with our belongings, as well as the things we had collected for Uganda in our travels. Instruments, including a piano, guitars, horns, drums, and a vibraharp. There was a travel trailer for us to work in with the pastors, as well as books, supplies for the Institute, and clothing. RUN also had finances to buy a car for Joshua and bicycles for the country pastors. We divided the other gifts with all the pastors. They were so thankful for the assistance. We began travelling, including crossing swamps. I remember the believers walking beside the vehicle and holding it so it wouldn't tip or sink. We went out to the Gospel Mission country churches with a pop-up tent trailer, along with interpreters and assistant teachers. Safaris included preaching, teaching, and dedicating babies, all in grass-roofed buildings, and eating their matoke, (made from the East African Highland banana) morning, noon and night. We would sing the old Sunday School song, slightly revised:

Matoke, matoke,
Matoke in the morning, motke in the noontime
Matoke, matoke
Matoke when the sun goes down!

I was interested to see my old Scandali accordion still being played! I had come with a beautiful new Italian accordion, a gift from the Yuba City church. RUN employed Wilfred, Joseph and Kaizi to help us. We began to help the Gospel Mission Bible School financially, and also started a Primary School.

This was an exciting time for Hugh and Audrey—their first visit since being expelled by the former dictator Idi Amin. Together we dedicated the Lake Victoria Full Gospel church in Entebbe. Our sister Ruth joined us. At this time Lew felt an urgency to register RUN Ministries with the Uganda government, and he did so. RUN rented a residence for the staff, where we also used the living room as an office.

We held our first Pastor's Conference in 1988 by renting the Makerere Universities Facility, and over 1000 Pastors attended.

The pastors of Bible Temple Portland, Glad Tidings Yuba City, and Glad Tidings Vancouver arrived, and we knew we were going to have a super time. The guest of honor was the Uganda Minister of Education. He encouraged us in our quest to begin much-needed schools.

After the conference, Pastor Iverson suggested RUN should look for property to bring the pastors in for teaching. That way, we also could do the training in practical ways for their families to earn income for survival. Also to build our homes on our own land would be somewhat easier on our health and our budget. Together we found and reserved a beautiful 20-acre piece of property on the shores of Lake Victoria at Bweranga village. Bible Temple helped us. We sold our car and raised the balance. We had to go back to the USA to maintain our resident status there, and also strengthen our financial base. The first Institute occurred while we were away, and we were thankful that Hugh remained in Uganda to conduct the first Institute, which included the men that we had hired, as well as some from the church who became our leadership team.

RBC

At this time we discovered that the blending of RUN with Gospel Mission was not going to work. It was difficult for them to change or add to their established history. This caused a huge upheaval in the total purpose of RUN Ministries and our existence in Uganda. However, God's plan came into view, and a church in Kampala emerged. We didn't plan it, and we were reminded of the prophetic word that came before we left the States. We were thankful that Hugh was there to "hold the fort" till we got back.

In Kampala, Run Bible Church began in Betty's Salon, then moved to an outdoor open amphitheater, then to the YMCA auditorium. After that a church in the USA donated a circus tent, so with permission we erected it on YMCA land at Wandegeya and began to expand outside of the Kampala and Uganda walls. Ministers

Fellowship International, East Africa (MFIEA) was established and grew. RUN now became "Reaching Unto Nations."

Meanwhile we had purchased land in Kampala to build a permanent building. Before we returned to the USA permanently, we cleared the land, burnt the foliage, broke the sod, dedicated the land, and began preparing it for the building.

The Layzells returned to Canada, and once again we began wearing three hats. RBC became the "horse" with the Institute and Pastor's Fellowship following in the cart. We knew this was God's plan. God does not have a plan "B" in our destiny when we serve Him faithfully. It is always plan "A". We just need to accept it, knowing He is in control.

Thieves

We had our share of thievery. During the wars it was an epidemic. At 7:00 in the evening you locked the doors and prayed! Any evening activity had to be over so that you got home no later than 7:00 p.m. At one point the army thieves were breaking into houses while the families were having dinner, and they would steal the dinner right off the table, always with their AK-47s in hand. Talk about a threat!

Our home was robbed three times—twice in Kampala and once in RUN Village. Once during the wars, the men that were living in our house took a Canadian flag and secured it to the roof so that when the army helicopters flew over the house, it might deter them from shooting over our house. We were also robbed in downtown Kampala. We had parked our pickup across from the post office, hid our shopping, and locked it securely. We were only gone but a few minutes and when we came back the doors were unlocked, our shopping bags were gone, and there were guys standing on the sidewalk watching us. Probably they were the thieves.

When peace, like a river, attendeth my way,
When sorrows like sea billows roll;
Whatever my lot, Thou hast taught me to say,

"It is well, it is well with my soul."
It is well with my soul.
It is well, it is well with my soul.
—Horatio G. Spafford (1836)

The Institute and Farm

We began to clear the institute land, with a team from Alberta that came to help. Lloyd came from Portland and built window and door frames. He also made a trip with us to Masaka, where we had the privilege of burning down a family witchcraft house that belonged to one the ladies in the church. She was the executor of the family's estate and had been delivered from demons, so she was out to destroy their authority over her. Lloyd had a good time beating at the flames, knocking down the walls as the "lubale" house burned.

We purchased a brick machine to begin making our own bricks. A church in England shipped us farm machinery. The dream slowly by slowly was coming to pass. We hired a bulldozer to help us clear the vines. They were strong enough to lift the front of the dozer up, but fortunately the cab had a roof, because on more than one occasion, snakes would fall out of the trees onto the dozer. Our closest neighbor was a shrine for witchcraft worship! Ken came from the USA, and we and the RBC congregation walked the perimeter of the land, cleansing it and dedication it to the Glory of God. Buy now we had a house staff and we all lived in Kampala. We had our share of miracles when building the Institute. On one of the trips over the lake to buy lumber, the group ended up in a storm on the way back. The lumber scattered, and our man was not a swimmer, so he hung on to the wood to keep afloat and did his best to gather the wood. Obviously, we lost on that trip, but they rescued some lumber and all were safe. Thank you, Jesus.

We moved onto the land as soon as we could. It was 20 acres of Jungle with "Tarzan" vines, hippos, crocodiles, snakes, vipers, ant bears, deer, monkeys, bugs and spiders. On that sandy shore and swamp, all of us were there together. I even had snakes in my house and had to call Anthony to kill them. He would break their back so they couldn't rise and strike. I didn't have the nerve—I just froze and yelled, "Anthony!" It was a great education for this city girl. The monkeys loved our vegetables and could wipe out a whole field of green peppers in no time. We had "Ganda" dogs, meaning dogs of no particular breed (mutts). They were almost wild themselves, but made great watchdogs, not fierce nor protective of us, but of the territory. They would take off after those monkeys and the monkeys would bolt, screaming as they scattered! The army ants were horrible and could they pinch. I have stripped more than once to pick them off my body while they left their pinchers in me. We woke up one morning and the bathtub was full of them. Hot water please!

Our staff, my sister Ruth, Larry and Carolyn and family (Bible Temple had financed a house for them) moved with us. We lived in our pop-up trailer and the staff lived in tents. We built the staff quarters first, and the latrines, as we didn't have running water—just the second largest inland lake in the world. We went to Entebbe to bring consumable water in jerry cans, washed clothes in the lake, and didn't have electricity.

When the staff quarters were livable, the staff moved, and we began building houses for our team as they married. At the same time we were building the Institute building and the chapel. Finally the builders began on our house. Imagine, to live in a house again instead of a tent trailer. Over a year had gone by living on the land. Those were rough days. I remember the frogs in our shower, and the tornado-force winds coming in off the lake (water spouts) that made us think we would blow away or drown.

Another miracle was when we were out of money and needed $10,000 to make the Institute building usable. We had the conference coming, and no roof on the building. Pastors were coming, and we had nowhere to put them where they could keep dry and protected. The students were staying in staff quarters where we had room for them. That morning when Lew was walking our watchdogs, he was crying out to the Lord (maybe complaining a little bit) when the

Lord told him, "Go back to the classroom where the pastors are praying. Give each one instructions to pray for a thousand dollars. Ten students = $ 10,000. They interceded with fervency. The next day there was a message for Lew to call Mari Lou in Portland, Oregon. He called, and she said, "Dad, guess what? I just received a check from an anonymous donor for $10,000! Lew just laughed and said, "Send it fast!" Then he told her of yesterday's experience. God is so good!

We employed a wonderful grounds caretaker, Anthony. He had his family with him, his wife, their five boys and two grown, married daughters. We became family. I still consider them my Ugandan family. They lived on the land, and we did so much together. They are all grown now, and have families of their own. Anthony lives out in the country on their own property. One of the daughters married our house manager, and they had two children, Peterson and Marion. Now to them I am "Grandma" and "Great-Grandma" to their kids. The youngest son, Emmanuel, is a pastor and has pioneered an amazing church near Kampala. When the boys were little they used to help me clean up the end cuts of the reeds from the making of the roof. We worked together for hours, loading the trailer behind the tractor.

The three youngest boys used to have church outside on the Institute land. Peterson would play the drums (tins and stumps), Amon would lead the worship and Emmanuel would preach. It was amazing to watch and listen to them. Today they are strong men and good fathers, still doing the same, in Emmanuel's Church!

> *I've got peace like a river, I've got peace like a river,*
> *I've got peace like a river in my soul. [2x]*
> *I've got joy like a fountain, I've got joy like a fountain,*
> *I've got joy like a fountain in my soul. [2x]*
> *—Traditional Spiritual*

I was destined to live in unfinished or wartorn houses for several years. None of the buildings was ever actually finished, just livable shells with cement floors, mud brick walls, thatched roof, doors and shutters. It was a happy day when we dug a well. No more pump, but we had running water when we ran for it!

The Institute was my joy. I loved teaching and writing the curriculum. I enjoyed visiting and having a cup of tea with the teachers that came out from Kampala. We also found great joy in having the pastors into our home just for tea and fun. The first Institute class was conducted by Hugh, the second was held in staff quarters while the Institute was being built, and the third was in the new Institute building.

The Institute operated three months on and one month off. We had three classes a year, depending on the applications. The plan was for a pastor to complete a three-month Institute class three times, which gave them a very concentrated time of study, learning practical ways to support their families. I don't know how many graduates completed the plan, as the records were left in Uganda. The average size of a three-month class was 15–20 pastors who already had a church in a village. They came from different organizations and neighboring countries. I would guess we had around 30 graduating classes. The teachers were RUN staff, RBC eldership and other Bible teachers and guests. How many did that three times, I don't know, but what I do know is that the pastors were very grateful for the training. We had hope that before we had to leave we would have enough trained teachers to have the three levels running simultaneously, but that did not happen.

Besides Bible, we taught planting and raising vegetables, which we sold to hotels in Kampala. The farm became a source of income for the Institute—not a lot, but every little bit helped. It also kept us in vegetables, and the lake had fish. We had a good supply of healthy food, and no western junk food. Leroy, Lisa and family spent some time with us and were a help in this farming challenge. Neither Lew nor I were farmers by any stretch of the imagination, so we appreciated all the help we could get. We raised rabbits, some chickens and Joseph's cows. Our goal was for the pastors to have a new zeal for reaching their villages for Jesus with understanding, and also to become independent financially. Lew brought and donated his extensive library collection from many years to the Institute.

MFI East Africa

The Ministers Fellowship just happened. Of course we know the Holy Spirit brought pastors to us, because word of God's happenings spread like wildfire. Early in RUN Ministries' journey, it became obvious that we needed to secure oversight. Soon after MFI (Ministers Fellowship International) began, we asked Pastor Iverson if RUN Ministries could join. He welcomed the brethren warmly, and we were happy, as our relationship with Bible Temple was longstanding. The Institute graduates and other pastors desired the help and security that MFI provided. We were members and desired to have our "baby" under the same covering. We tried to have a regular Regional Conference, as well as one General Conference a year, but finances and lack of dependable vehicles at times hindered that fulfillment.

In 2018 I visited again, joining in the celebration of 30 years of RUN Ministries in Uganda. It is now called Life Church, but it is the same ministry, with lots and lots of new faces. The beautiful building is a tribute to all who worked so hard on it. Bob and Sharon Wagar followed us after some previous shaky months and accomplished an indescribable forward move in the church. We were privileged to lay a strong foundation, then what they built upon that is just thrilling.

God's Vision

RUN Ministries is God's vision. It is not the Petersons' or City Bible Church's, but God's! We were only facilitators for His vision. He said He had a plan that we didn't even know, so we have to believe that despite all the human mistakes, He is in control, and He has orchestrated all that has occurred.

We fulfilled our calling and passed the initial fulfillment of the vision on to the national leaders. Bob and Sharon continued with excellence, and the national leaders are carrying on in that vision (which is now theirs) with excellence and are training and next generation under them.

To fulfill the second phase of the vision will require persons with:

- Holy Spirit sensitivity
- Building knowledge
- Experience in developing and property planning
- Knowledge in investment principles, business and micro-lending
- Contacts for financial assistance
- The gift of teaching
- Gifts of Administration

This we will do as God permits (see Hebrews 6:3). "The vision will not tarry" any longer! The vision will come to pass.

Looking Back

As Lew and I prepared to write this book, we decided to say it like it is. That can be dangerous, but that is who we are.

Obviously we were not perfect, but with that, ministry wise, we had one major weakness that in our position in carrying out God's purpose for RUN Ministries was obvious. We had no knowledge on how to raise money! We were not promoters. We loved doing the job, but we didn't know how to raise the money to support the job. We tried, but the gifting was not there.

Lew's philosophy was that you are not a success if you do not have a successor. We raised successors, and laid a foundation that is still strong today. We had no trouble welcoming help in areas that we knew were weak in. So many folk helped us and we are so grateful. If it wasn't for your help, then we would not have had the privilege of laying such a solid foundation. But we failed in being able to teach how to promote the need and raise money to pay for it without feeling like we were begging. It was not difficult for us to promote the gospel or present day truth, but if we had hired someone to handle the natural part of promotion, then a lot of unnecessary stress would have been avoided. As church pastors, often we don't know the inner working of the promotional world. Lessons have to be learned and we learned ours, a little late but nevertheless we learned.

- Honor the Past
- Experience the Present
- Embrace the Future

This is an exhortation Lew wrote about seven years ago.

The years go by...the energy diminishes...the body weakens and the days seem to go by faster. As Pastors of a past generation living in the present, but looking forward to the future, we have learned that we cannot live in the past nor in the hope of the future. Every new day is the present and a fulfillment of the future. We must not be sad or discouraged, thinking we are useless, but come alongside the new generation to help them finish the job. It is their turn now!

> "...since we are surrounded by so great a cloud of witnesses,
> let us lay aside every weight, and the sin which
> so easily ensnares us,
> and let us run with endurance the race that is set before us,
> looking unto Jesus, the author and finisher of our faith,
> who for the joy that was set before Him endured the cross,
> despising the shame, and has sat down
> at the right hand of the throne of God."
> —Hebrews 12:1, 2

The past years of the Church in East Africa have been glorious. Men and women who are now in their senior years were mightily used of God to lay a foundation for the church of today. They must be continually honored. We will honor and remember them and their pioneer labor given to the today generation to build upon. David served his generation according to the will of God and recognized it was now the new generation's turn to build on the foundation. Solomon's turn! We remember and honor the revivals and refreshing, the awesome outpouring of the Holy Spirit in our lives that began the Pentecostal experience across the region. Hundreds of local churches sprang up, and young pastors learned to lead the people of God. We don't throw the foundation away, but build on it. They were thrilling days, but the church can't live in the foundation. We must live today with the message of today. We are building a house—God's house!

There is now a *present* word for the church in East Africa. Make a decision to be persistent. Jesus, for the joy set before Him, salvation for the entire world, endured the cross on that glorious day. He rose again three days later to present the *now Word* for that generation. Identify what hinders you from enjoying your present. Is it fear of failure, the economy, wounds, emotions, personality, relationships, circumstances, or hardships? Bring those situations to Jesus. Trust Him. He called you, and He will perform all that concerns you and your calling. Fix your focus on what His purpose is for today. Draw from mentors, find a catalyst that will lift your spirit and encourage you, and enter every day with joy and anticipation.

Embrace the future, whatever it holds. That is your hope. Hope establishes your faith to embrace the future. We don't know what the future holds, but we know who holds the future.

What a treasure I have in this wonderful peace
Buried deep in the heart of my soul,
So secure that no power can mine it away,
While the years of eternity roll!

I am resting tonight in this wonderful peace,
Resting sweetly in Jesus' control;
For I'm kept from all danger by night and by day,
And His glory is flooding my soul!

Peace, peace, wonderful peace,
Coming down from the Father above!
Sweep over my spirit forever I pray,

In fathomless billows of love!
—*W. G. Cooper (1889)*

Here Am I, Lord. Send me!

The Need (see Luke 11:21, 22)

- The local church is the spawning ground for world missions
- All church leaders need to recognize we are in the springtime of world missions
- An awareness of what God is doing in missions in our day
- A willingness to become involved in ongoing missions as a local church
- Commitment to spiritual warfare to bind the strong man

The Vision (see Proverbs 29:18)

People will perish if the church doesn't rise to spread the Gospel.

The Field (see Matthew 13:37, 38)

- The whole world: wayside, stony ground, thorny ground, and good ground!
- Don't observe the wind. You won't sow (see Ecclesiastes 11:1–4).
- Don't observe the clouds. You won't reap.

The Seed (see Mark 4:14)

The Word of God

The Harvest (see Matthew 9:37, 38)

- Plenteous
- Problem: lack of laborers
- Solution: Pray that the Lord of the harvest will send out laborers.

The Method

- Make Disciples (see Matthew 28:19)
- Sending Principle (see Romans 10:14, 15)
- Ask: Who will go? (see Isaiah 6:1–8)
- Long term and Short term
- Everyone: be a sender, or be sent
- Do what you can. (see Mark 14:18)

The Local Church

- God's vehicle
- Gifted ministry (see Ephesians 4:11–13)
- Excellent administration (see Corinthians 8:15–24)
- Known ministers (see 1 Thessalonians 5:12, 13)
- Possess potential for lasting results

The Result

- It works (see Revelation 5:8–14)
- Kindred, Tongue, People and Nation (see Revelation 7:9–12)

During my visit to Uganda in 2018 to celebrate the 30th anniversary of RUN Bible Church and Ministries (Life Church), the leaders presented me with a beautiful album of the history of the ministry. It contains pictures, names, and the story of every step we made to lay the foundation of the ministry, from the beginning in

1988 to 1997, and then on to 2018. The following are the words of the last page written to us.

> Thank you for the years you and Pastor Peterson poured into the foundation of Life Church. Those years went into the forming of a group of young (now much older people) that have over the years been pivotal in the preservation of the House of God called Life Church. The vision that you and Pastor Lew received from God was and still is a far reaching vision in its impact on the lives of those who have gone before, but all those that are coming ahead.
>
> We are honored to be part of the laboring force that God has so graciously asked to move this vision forward. We pray that the latter years of your life will be filled with the Lord's presence, grace and provision. We celebrate you and honor your labor among us.
>
> We love you and are glad you could come.
>
> **Richard and Dora Senkungu**
>
> "And I will give you shepherds after my own heart, who will feed you with knowledge and understanding" (Jeremiah 3:15).
>
> **Thank you for shepherding Life Church.**

> *Grace, Grace, God's Grace*
> *Marvelous grace of our loving Lord,*
> *Grace that exceeds our sin and our guilt,*
> *Yonder on Calvary's mount outpoured,*
> *There where the blood of the Lamb was spilt.*

> *Sin and despair like the sea waves cold,*
> *Threaten the soul with infinite loss;*
> *Grace that is greater, yes, grace untold,*
> *Points to the Refuge, the mighty Cross.*

> *Dark is the stain that we cannot hide,*
> *What can avail to wash it away?*

Look! There is flowing a crimson tide;
Whiter than snow you may be today.

Marvelous, infinite, matchless grace,
Freely bestowed on all who believe;
You that are longing to see His face,
Will you this moment His grace receive?

Grace, grace, God's grace,
Grace that will pardon and cleanse within;
Grace, grace, God's grace,
Grace that is greater than all our sin.
—Daniel B. Towner and Julia Johnston (1911)

Run Bible Church Leadership Staff

Surveying, Clearing the Land and Laying Brick

Ministers Fellowship East Africa

Kenya

Nigeria

Botswana

Ghana

Congo

Pretoria, South Africa

Mwanza, Tanzania

CHAPTER NINE

Run, Sheep, Run

*I*t was a sunny afternoon at youth camp in July, 1953, and it was free time to play. Our team was hunkered down behind a log in the woods, hiding from the opposing team. Our team leader was out with the other team, trying to lead them away from where we were hiding. We could hear him calling out our signals, warning us how far or close they were to finding us. We knew he had drawn a map in the dirt on the ball field showing them where we were—sort of! We waited, holding our breath and listening, they were getting closer. Then we heard the signal, "Run, Sheep, Run," and we bolted out and raced the other team to the ball field to rub out the map.

What a wonderful illustration of Jesus' love for today's generation. The enemy is looking for them, he has seen the map and is trying to find them, to destroy them and win. Our leader, Jesus, is calling out signals to let them know just where he is, so that when he gets too close, hopefully they will hear Jesus' call in time: "Run, Sheep, Run." Get out of the dark woods, resist the temptation, and run for your life back into His safety and His presence.

I have left this chapter until last because of my love and vision for the next generation. I served the Lord in my youth, what seems like a long time ago, and now I am old. But I have always had a passion, and it has not changed:

> **Without the youth in our churches,**
> **we have no hope for the future.**

For this final chapter I have gone through 60 years of message notes and teachings by Lew and me. Hopefully they will be valuable to the next generation. Some of our strategies are in lists, some are the principal scriptures that guided our steps, and others are discussions of how we approached serving the Lord. If you are inspired and want to use any of the thoughts, you are welcome. His Word is our foundation.

When I was in Uganda in 2018, I sat with a group of young adult men who had not been true disciples of Jesus for very long. They expressed their desire to serve Jesus with enthusiasm and zeal, while juggling the responsibilities of a job, marriage, raising a family, and living for Jesus in a world that is uncertain and at times politically difficult. They asked me, "How did you do it? You raised a strong church, our leaders were young then, and war was all around you. Yet they married, their wives and all their kids are now in the church, and some married and have children. It is amazing. How? Did you choose wives for them? How did you do it?"

I replied, "I don't know! No, we did not choose their brides. We just put one step in front of another and moved forward. We never thought about it, we just did whatever came our way, as the Holy Spirit directed us."

I am so grateful for their hunger to be and do all that the Lord wants. God gave them the ability to make choices, and the presence of the Holy Spirit in their lives to make the right ones. They just have to listen.

God created us with the power of choice. Every choice we make in life is accompanied by this question: How much pain or pleasure is this going to cost me? If there is not significant effort or discomfort associated with the process, we will not appreciate the delight.

Pleasure / Pain Principle

It is amazing to me that God gives a choice between being blessed or cursed. Imagine, God has the power to do anything He wants, and yet He allows us to choose what we want! Do I want to disobey Him, or obey Him? It is my choice.

> **Blessing . . . Joy . . . Obey**
> —Deuteronomy 28:1–14
>
> **Cursing . . . Pain . . . Disobey**
> —Deuteronomy 28:15–54

God is serious. To Him this is serious, eternal business. Joy is waiting. Seeing beyond the pain.

> " . . . looking unto Jesus, the author and finisher of our faith,
> who for the joy that was set before Him endured the cross,
> despising the shame, and has sat down
> at the right hand of the throne of God."
> —Hebrews 12:2

Many times I have had to use Jesus' experience to give myself a mental checkup. Imagine if He had not suffered for me. What would my suffering feel like? I am usually a positive person. While pain is not my thing, I do want to grow and become mature. I want to be part of the Bride that He suffered the pain for. God's discipline is painful but loving, painful but merciful, painful but gracious. How do we learn to accept the pain?

> "For consider Him who endured such hostility
> from sinners against Himself,
> lest you become weary and discouraged in your souls."
> —Hebrews 12:3

We Learn from Experience (see Psalm 51:10–13)

Like King David we must learn our need . . .

- for a clean heart
- for a renewed, steadfast spirit
- for God's presence
- for the Holy Spirit
- for the joy of God's salvation
- to be upheld by God's generous Spirit

This will result in . . .

- the ability to teach others
- sinners will be converted

Repulsive Images, Impacting Testimonies

The process is usually one of self discipline, as I make decisions both naturally and spiritually. I need to reach the point where I decide, "I am not going to allow anything to short-circuit my life and rob me of my destiny." What good is a fleeting pleasure when the pain and guilt will rob you of your relationship with God? Your choices determine everything: your conduct, your character and your future.

Today's generation faces a great dilemma. It is an "as you like it" generation. It is "all about me." There are no more social standards to guide them. If the home upholds moral standards, then society, the education authorities, the entertainment idols, as well as the athletic heroes mock them. In my day all of those groups had standards, and the standards were not considered to be religious or ethnic, but the right way to live. That is all gone, and the youth are lost in indecision. It is time to get up and Run, Sheep, Run!

Here are some vital factors for young people to consider as they grow into adults with responsibilities and work out their destiny.

1. **Emotions — Not Allowing My Feelings to Control Me**

   "Let not your Heart be troubled." (John 14:1)
   "Set your affection on things above." (Colossians 3:2)

2. **Questions — To Find the Best Answers, Ask the Right Questions**

   How much will this cost me?

   What is the downside?

   Is this compatible with my destiny?

3. **Mentors — Need for a Life Coach**

   My decisions will improve, because of the sense of responsibility I feel.

4. **Data Bank — Knowledge is Power**

   Whoever spends just *thirty minutes a day* studying a particular topic will become among the world's leading authorities on that subject within their lifetime.

5. **Value System — Ethics and Morals Matter**

   I must make my choices with prayer and make them permanent. What do I feel in my heart about this matter? Would this choice be contrary to my commitment to the Lord? "Thy word have I hid in mine heart, that I might not sin against thee" (Psalm 119:19).

Seeing is Believing

Do you see what I am saying? Words are abstract. You can never say it unless you envision it. It is your mental image that produces the words. We say exactly what we see. When God births something in my spirit, I don't have to read it, just describe it and meditate on the Word until it becomes alive, creating pictures in my mind, soul and heart. Remember this: What God shows you in heaven, He will confirm on earth.

Visualize It

Don't just verbalize it. Visualize it! You will never rise above the pictures that are engraved on your mind. What will it be? Do you have an image of what the Lord desires for you? If your body is sick, you must see yourself well. If my wallet is empty, I must see it full. Stop dwelling on what is. Get a new picture. If you only dwell on what already exists, you will miss what God wants to bring into reality.

Written Strategy

Decide how you will overcome the problem. Write down your goal and a plan to achieve it. You don't have the chance to exercise personal discipline unless your future is more important than your present circumstances. The goal in front of you must take precedence over the temptation that is after you. Don't switch gears and reverse. Your past is not more attractive than your future.

> "Those things, which ye have both learned and received
> and heard and seen in me, do:
> and the God of peace shall be with you."
> —Philippians 4:9

- Think it!
- Learn it!
- Receive it!
- Hear it!
- See it!
- Do it!

As a youth 67 years ago, who wanted to serve God and fulfill her destiny, here was my formula:

> "I have *chosen* the way of truth;
> your judgments I have laid before me.

I *cling* to your testimonies; O Lord, don't put me to shame!
I have *run* the course of your commandments,
for you shall enlarge my heart."
—Psalm 119:30–32

1. **I made my *choice*.**

   He had chosen me! "Just as He chose us in Him before the foundation of the world that we should be holy and without blame before Him in love." (Ephesians 1:4).

2. **I decided to *cling*.**

   I will hold my confidence as long as I live. "For as we have become partakers of Christ if we hold the beginning of our confidence to the end" (Hebrews 3:14).

3. **I will *run*.**

   Move forward. I will not stand still or be dragged along by someone else. "Do you not know that those who run in a race all run, but one receives the prize? Run in such a way that you may obtain it. Therefore I run thus, not with uncertainty, but I discipline my body and bring it into subjection, lest, when I have preached to others I myself should become disqualified" (1 Corinthians 9:24–27).

RUN, Sheep, RUN!

There is a saying, "Never say Never." We are human, and our life situations change, and we don't want to have to "eat our words!" In the process of living, we must always keep moving. When I leave the doctor's office at this season of my life, he says, "Keep moving, Marion." With the arthritis, that is a tall order. The old body wants to sit, rest, and move slowly, but the effort made to keep going will keep me useful and alive. Here are some truths about our Lord that never change, and I must keep them before me. Remembering them will bolster my trust in Him through the hard times.

A message for the young from the old is to remember the attributes of God that He freely lets us hang on to, sometimes for dear life.

- He *never* fails.
- He *never* leaves or forsakes us.
- He *never* refuses to fulfill His word.
- He *never* neglects to hear our prayers and petitions.
- He *never* lies.
- He *never* slumbers or sleeps.
- He *never* worries.

Keep your eyes on the road. Look straight ahead. The vision is before you. Here are some "nevers" as shared by my friend, Pastor Derrill Corbin. Let us remember these as we live out our testimony to the new generation finding their way on the path of life. Run, Sheep, Run!

- Never allow the world, the flesh or the devil to shape your vision, for vision shapes your destiny.
- Never allow smallness of vision, or thinking, or smallness of what "is" today to rule your life.
- Never allow those who have no faith to influence you.
- Never allow discouragement to dominate your faith in God's ability to fulfill your dream and vision.
- Never allow circumstances to limit your vision. Change your circumstances through faith.
- Never allow finances to become the dictator of vision. God is your source.
- Never allow failure to set your course in life. Get up and try again, and have a faith that never gives up!

"For it is God who works in you
both to will and to do for His good pleasure."
—Philippians 2:13

Courage

There is arising around us in this generation a crowd of courageous Christian youth. No doubt about it, the Godly youth of today must be courageous. There are numerous attacks on every aspect of their lives.

What does courage mean? The ability to conquer fear or despair; bravery; full of valor; a quality or temperament that enables one to stand fast in the face of opposition, hardship or danger. (Synonyms: dauntlessness, fearlessness; guts, heart resolution, spirit, spunk; the opposite of cowardice.)

When I need courage, God is my source. Everything else is a resource. I must never treat the resource as a source, because the resource will strangle me. Why? Because courage requires faith that God is with me, and He helps me in a time of need!

> *Be of good courage,*
> **in spite of the conditions you see.**

"Teach me Your way, O Lord,
And lead me in a smooth path, because of my enemies.
Do not deliver me to the will of my adversaries;
For false witnesses have risen against me,
And such as breathe out violence.
I would have lost heart, unless I had believed
That I would see the goodness of the Lord
In the land of the living.
Wait on the Lord; Be of good courage,
And He shall strengthen your heart;
Wait, I say on the Lord!"
—Psalm 27:11–14

My Father used to remind us that, "Any dead fish can flow with the current. It takes a live, healthy fish to swim upstream." Where were the fish going? To the spawning grounds for reproduction. It takes courage to keep going when the going gets tough, but if I want to reproduce true disciples for His kingdom, sometimes I have to go against the current, keep believing, and fight for new life.

In order to be courageous, I have to continually strengthen myself. How? By prayer, Bible reading, praying in the spirit, right fellowship, godly friends, and participation with a gathering of believers. In 2 Chronicles 32 we find these exhortations:

- Rebuild my walls, raise up towers, build a "second wall"
- Set my weapons in order
- Be part of the warriors
- Be an encourager
- Don't be afraid or dismayed
- Know that God is with me
- God will help me fight the battles

Generations

Moses sent spies into Canaan to spy it out, and to determine how they would conquer the land. After the spies came back from Canaan, all but two allowed discouragement to overtake them. Joshua and Caleb said, "No way. We are well able to take the land." Why did they have a different report than the other spies? Because there was a different spirit within them. They encouraged the other spies, but to no avail. Forty years later, every member of that generation had died except Joshua and Caleb, who went into the Promised Land for their inheritance. The new generation conquered Canaan.

As they were preparing to conquer Canaan, God (through Moses and Joshua) told the new generation: Be strong and of good courage. The Lord will fight your battles. Joshua is the one who goes before you to lead you. Do not fear. The inheritance will be divided for each one. The Lord will be with you wherever you go. We will take the land together, and the Lord will take care of all your enemies against whom you fight.

Here are some interesting thoughts:

- Man is interested in Congregations.
- God is interested in Generations.
- The Church of Jesus Christ is always only one generation away from extinction.

> "Joseph and all His generation died,
> but the children of Israel were fruitful and increased
> abundantly, multiplied and grew exceedingly mightily;
> and the land was filled with them."
> —Exodus 1:7

God is in the business of destroying His enemies from one generation to another. The only way each generation will win is if the older generation passes on the news. God is for us. This is what has happened in the past. The only hitch is that each generation must listen and learn. There are always new methods, but the conquering method never changes. Pass on the truth, the victories, and the pain—everything the old generation has experienced and conquered. Then it is the new generation's job to add to it!

> "Hear this, you elders, and give ear,
> all you inhabitants of the land!
> Has anything like this happened in your days,
> or even in the days of your fathers?
> Tell your children about it,
> Let your children tell their children,
> and their children another generation."
> —Joel 1:2, 3

The devil thinks this is his land, and he is fighting and doing everything he can to stop me from my destiny. This is the season of the prophetic and apostolic, to enable every saint to fulfill their destiny. The devil has had his day—he is history. I am on the winning team. My success, and the fulfillment of my destiny, is in the next generation.

"Who knows the spirit of the sons of men,
which goes upward,
and the spirit of the animal, which goes down to the earth?
So I perceived that nothing is better than that a man should
rejoice in his own works, for that is his heritage.
For who can bring him to see what will happen after him?"
—Ecclesiastes: 21, 22

Humans are different than animals, trees, birds, bugs, etc., that cannot make choices. They have neither inheritance nor heritage. They have instincts, but cannot make plans and goals for themselves or their families. We make choices that affect the value of our lives, and the best choice is to do what you can rejoice in. That is what you will pass on to the next generation, and what they will seek to do in their generation.

Good and Bad Heritage

Reject it or accept it. Israel had a problem. They forsook their inheritance, which opened the door for the enemy to destroy them and take them into bondage.

Rejoice in your own works? You will never know what will happen after you are gone. Do what is best with your heritage, so that you can be proud to pass it on. Earthly heritage is yours, whether you like it or not. It is possible to mess up and lose one's inheritance. Wait for maturity. Make a way for you and for your children.

Benefits of a Good Heritage
- Wealthy
- Love and acceptance
- Property
- Family tradition
- Political
- Business

- Intelligence
- Genetic
- Faith

Lew and I thank God for our natural heritage. We both had awesome parents, who taught us to be good citizens, honest and responsible. They also established us firmly in our faith, which has carried us through the good and bad times. What did we inherit? We are not going to remember the negative traits.

Marion's Heritage

My whole life I was reminded, "You are like your father." How I hated that. I did not want to be like my Father! Yet I did inherit his abilities in leadership, pioneering, creativity, administration, music, public speaking, and a positive faith. I had to learn how to live with these comments. Oh, help! Anyway, we will not go there.

Lew's Heritage

Lew was proud to be like his father. He inherited a hard-working ethic and a pioneering spirit. He was a calculator, a counselor, musical, caring, and an outstanding public speaker with a strong conviction of faith.

However, God doesn't look at this. These traits were automatically ours through our natural physical birth. God uses our natural characteristics for the good of His kingdom, but what we do with it is up to us, and that is not an eternal issue. God looks at what we are doing with our Spiritual Heritage. Spiritual Heritage by Eternal Life Birth is for now and forever.

Humanity has an enemy that desires to "steal, kill and destroy" man's spiritual heritage. He is called Satan, and his works infiltrate the hearts and minds of human beings, drawing them away from what God wants us to inherit.

Heritage is God's plan, which He promised to Moses when He delivered the Israelites from Pharaoh. Israel and Egypt were the ancient equivalents to the Christian church today, versus the ungodly culture of the secular world. However, they had their problems with maintaining and maturing into God's provision for them.

> "And you, even yourself shall let go of your
> heritage which I gave you;
> and it will cause you to serve your enemies
> in the land which you do not know;
> for you have kindled a fire in my anger,
> which will burn forever."
> —Jeremiah 17:4

Even in spiritual, eternal heritage, mankind has choices.

- Reject it or accept it. Understand its eternal value.
- Can you rejoice in your own works?
- You will never know what will happen to it after you are gone.
- Do a good job with your eternal heritage so you would be proud of the following generations, because they *will* follow you.
- Heritage is yours, whether you want it or not. Receive it and appreciate it.
- One can mess up and lose it.
- The full inheritance comes with maturity in our walk with Jesus.
- By the way we handle our inheritance, we show the way for generations following to continue in the good inheritance.

This eternal heritage is for every person ever born on earth. It is our choice. Each person must make his or her own choice. It is mine by birth into Jesus' family. Accept it and live by His standards. Obey the criteria He has given to qualify for your inheritance.

Live by faith, follow His guidelines, and the enjoy the righteous heritage that is available to you, which is eternal life. Live forever with the God who birthed you into His family through His Son.

If anyone rejects the offer of their eternal heritage and then realizes what they have done, they can change their mind, ask for forgiveness, and be welcomed into the Kingdom. The inheritance still belongs to them, because they have returned to be part of the family. It is ours to keep for now and all Eternity. Amazing.

"Blessed be the God and Father of our Lord Jesus Christ,
who according to His abundant mercy has begotten us again
to a living hope through the resurrection of
Jesus Christ from the dead,
to an inheritance incorruptible and undefiled
and that does not fade away,
reserved in heaven for you, who are kept by the power of God
through faith for salvation ready to be
revealed in the last time."
—1 Peter 1:3–5

Benefits

"The lines have fallen to me in pleasant places;
Yes, I have a good inheritance."
—Psalm 16:6

"He has declared to His people the power of His works,
in giving them the heritage of the nations."
— Psalm 111:6

"Behold, children are a heritage from the Lord,
the fruit of the womb is a reward."
—Psalm 127:3

"And whatever you do, do it heartily as to
the Lord and not to men,
knowing that from the Lord you will receive

the reward of the inheritance;
for you serve the Lord Christ."
— Colossians 2:23, 24

It is so easy. Believe by faith, because the will is already written. Accept it and believe it. It is yours! Jesus said: "Do not fear," for it is your Father's good pleasure to give you His Kingdom. It is your inheritance for eternity—everlasting life!

Liberty

"Give me liberty, or give me death!" is a quotation attributed to Patrick Henry from a speech he made to the Virginia Convention in 1775, at St. John's Church in Richmond, Virginia.

"Those who deny freedom to others
deserve it not for themselves."
—Abraham Lincoln

"While we shall negotiate freely,
we shall not negotiate freedom."
—J. F. Kennedy

We humans have always been desperate to be free, to be at liberty to do and be whatever we desire. What is the source of true freedom?

"For the law of the Spirit of life in Christ Jesus
has made me free from the law of sin and death."
—Romans 8:2

God has given us an open door to enter into freedom. The question is, "Do I really want to be free?" If so, He gives freedom to every man if he asks. It is a gift! It is so simple and wonderful. *True freedom* is only found in Jesus. Then Jesus asks us to share our freedom with others who are searching for lasting and authentic *freedom*.

"Heal the sick, cleanse the lepers,
raise the dead, cast out demons.
Freely you have received, freely give."
—Matthew 10:8

Overwhelmed

Our 2014 visit in Uganda was very different for us than any other time we have visited, since last being there in 2008. First, because our grandsons Ed and Brian were with us. Second, because we didn't go to minister in a conference, but to visit with our friends, students and other folk we had ministered with and to in years past. It was amazing as we "ran into" friends seemingly by chance! Gary and Marilyn Skinner in the passport lineup; Pastor Agatha; RUN's secretary Ruth Namattiti; and many others.

We accompanied Pastor Joseph to an MFI regional conference in the Masaka District, where we enjoyed time with many RUN Institute alumni. Such a joy! There was much said that warmed our hearts and overwhelmed us again and again. So many gracious and thankful folk expressed their love and appreciation to us for the years of teaching and living with them, which had established a firm foundation in every aspect of their lives, bringing *freedom* to them as they continued to increase in their destiny through the years.

Fulfillment

Since our grandsons' births while we lived in Uganda, the folk there had seen pictures of them and had heard all the grandparent stories. We had a dream that one day we would go to Uganda with them, and 2014 was the year of that fulfillment. Ed and Brian are now young men in their 20's, and both are dedicated to the destiny God has chosen for them. Fulltime ministry is the desire of their hearts. Their girlfriends (now they both are married) asked to go along on the trip, and we agreed. My, oh my! What a great time they all had! We watched, listened and said, "Amena!" to all the ministry the "four-some" did together.

They preached, sang and led worship, played their guitars, had an outreach basketball clinic, shared in the intern classes, and made a trip to the Sesse Islands to preach at a Pastor's conference. They preached at the Pastor's MFI Regional, and in general enjoyed every moment of ministry. There are too many stories. The trip to the source of the Nile; and the canoe ride and walk (in the water) out to where Lake Victoria drops a foot to flow into the Nile; the thunderstorm that blew down their tent; the long rides through "jams" in the traffic on the roads with crater-like potholes; the "border borders" (motorcycles) that zigzag through the traffic with no regard for anyone or anything; the "rescue" zoo with two white Rhinos (endangered species); crossing the Equator; and more! We all came home with grateful hearts. Tired? Yes! But ever so thankful for His protection and blessing.

"Stand fast therefore in the liberty by which
Christ has made us free,
and do not be entangled again with a yoke of bondage."
—Galatians 5:1

Your freedom in Jesus is contagious. Infect someone else with it and the infection will spread until all will experience the LIBERTY that there is in accepting Jesus's free gift, *true freedom.*

Some time ago, we received a thought from our "Granddaughter" in Uganda: "God will never be predictable or controllable, but always trustworthy! View matters you cannot understand as divine mysteries and things too wonderful for you to know."

"See, I am doing a new thing!
Now it springs up: do you not perceive it?
I am making a way in the desert and
streams in the wasteland."
—Isaiah 43:19

When I was committed to the workings of God in my life, I found true Joy—not earthly happiness but true, godly joy. If my happiness in earthly circumstances disappeared, all I had to do was plug into His everlasting, unspeakable joy.

It is joy unspeakable and full of glory,
Full of glory, full of glory,
It is joy unspeakable and full of glory,
Oh, the half has never yet been told.

I have found the pleasure I once craved,
It is joy and peace within;
What a wondrous blessing, I am saved
From the awful gulf of sin.
—B. E. Warren, 1900

"Don't you know that day dawns after night,
showers displace drought,
and spring and summer follow winter?
Then, have hope! Hope forever, for God will not fail you!"
—Charles Spurgeon

Through the years of his ministry, I remember my father being influenced by the writings of Charles Spurgeon and quoting from his teachings. Because of Dad's influence Lew began a collection of Charles Spurgeon's books. As a result, his sermons had an influence on the foundation of our basic Christian walk through the years.

Years ago Uncle George, Dad's youngest brother, made a search of our family heritage and discovered that Charles Spurgeon was my great-grandfather's pastor. In 1890, when in his youth, my Grandfather Arthur was not serving the Lord, and Spurgeon wrote him a letter pleading with him to turn to the Lord.

Spurgeon wrote a challenging letter to Arthur. Listen to a few of his words:

Dear Arthur Layzell,

I was a little while ago at a meeting for prayer where a number of ministers were gathered together, the subject of prayer was "our children" . . . I thought, I will write to those sons and daughters, and remind them of their parents' prayers . . . come and tell Jesus you have sinned; seek forgiveness; trust in Him for it and be sure that you are saved . . . I pray you think of heaven and hell; for in one of those places you will live forever. Meet me in heaven! Meet me at once at the mercy seat.

Yours very lovingly,

C.H. Spurgeon

As a result of this letter Spurgeon led Arthur to the Lord, and he later attended Spurgeon's College, then Pastor's College. This was an amazing discovery for us and brought understanding to Dad's attraction to the writings of Spurgeon, and his firm fundamental beliefs.

We are now in 2019, and looking back over the years I am reminded of the words of David.

"He remembers His covenant forever,
the word which He commanded, for a thousand generations"
—Psalm 105:8

God has always been more interested in generations than congregations. Today, I am thankful for my generational heritage, knowing of seven generations of our family line who have and are continuing to pass on the message of the gospel. Many have believed because of the faith and confidence of parents and pastors who believed, prayed and passed on truth. Every grandparent and parent of every family is authorized by heaven itself to pass on and guide each generation into the glorious truth of salvation, walking with the Lord their entire life, passing truth to their their children, and guiding them to walk confidently into their destiny.

"The steps of a good man are ordered by the Lord,
and he delights in his way.
Though he fall, he shall not be utterly cast down;
for the Lord upholds him with His hand."
—Psalm 37:23, 24

We can trust Him even though we don't understand the moment. He allows us to choose our path and then He guides every footstep along that path. Let Him surprise you. May your hope, prayers, and beliefs be strengthened daily as you fulfill your destiny, passing on truth and guiding the next generation through the mysteries of life, following Jesus and praising Him for every victory! Our hope is in Him!

Contentment

Be godly, and be content to *be* and *do* what God has for me—not lazy, but content in my place of action.

This generation of godly youth has a purpose in the kingdom for this time. Being godly is important, but we must partner godliness together with *being content where God has us.* We are in a process as we move toward our destiny.

This is accomplished through rejoicing, gentleness, and being anxious for nothing. Through prayer and supplication, with thanksgiving, make your requests known, and the peace of God will guard your heart. Meditate on these things. Learn, receive, hear, see, do, and be content in who and what you are in God.

"Not that I speak in regard to need,
for I have learned in whatever state I am, to be content."
—Philippians 4:11

"Now godliness with contentment is great gain."
—1 Timothy 6:6

Infusion

I am "Tea Granny"! I love my tea, and it has to be made properly. You can blame my British-born mother for that! First, it has to be made with freshly boiled water, not just hot water. The tea must be infused. It cannot be in a tea bag, as that contains it. It must float to be infused. Second, the pot or the cup (not a coffee mug) has to be warmed. Third, the best tea is loose tea, not a tea bag. If milk is used, it should be warm and in the cup first, so when the tea is poured from the teapot into the cup, it cooks the milk. So said Nellie Horrox Layzell.

Our spirit needs to be infused with the Holy Spirit, so we will have the boldness to move around and see God change peoples' lives. Taste, and see that the Lord is good!

May this generation rise up to be part of the greatest display of power by true disciples of Jesus Christ.

> *I have decided to follow Jesus,*
> *I have decided to follow Jesus,*
> *I have decided to follow Jesus.*
> *No turning back, no turning back.*
> *If none go with me, still I will follow,*
> *If none go with me, still I will follow.*
> *If none go with me, still I will follow,*
> *No turning back, no turning back.*
> —S. S. Singh (Public Domain)

During our years of ministry responsibilities at Vancouver Glad Tidings Temple, we had several teens join our family for short or long seasons. At different times we were asked if my niece and two nephews could come and be with us, in order to continue their education, while Hugh and Audrey remained in Uganda. We were surprised but honored to help in any way we could. We knew this would be difficult for all of them. We enjoyed having them with us. Imagine: all three were married out of our home, and that was a great honor for us.

Then came Jenny, a troubled girl who had gone astray and needed a steady home atmosphere to turn her around. Lew said so many times, "Into every home a little Jenny must come!" Because we had never had a teen problem in the house before, it was a learning curve for us. It was not smooth sailing, but we are all still alive to tell the tale! Jenny conveys her love and thanks, as she always remembers our birthdays, anniversaries, Christmas, as well as sending pictures and emails from time to time.

Darlene was not a teen. She became a friend to me and a big sister to Mari Lou. She arrived as a young adult, having crossed Canada by train, dressed in her overalls and with her guitar over her shoulder—a very talented young woman. She was a Jesus believer, but wanted to learn more about His ways. I don't remember how she found Glad Tidings, but there she was. Youth camp was just around the corner, and we had been asking for a lifeguard. She volunteered, and we were amazed. God brought her to us just when we needed her, and it turned out that she needed us. We did four weeks of camp together. She was everything she had claimed to be, and we bonded as friends. After camp we invited her to live with us, which she did, and we all loved having her in our home.

That summer our family did a road trip south to visit the Hamons in Texas. Darlene and Jenny went along with us, which added flavor to the trip. Darlene married a young man who received Jesus in Glad Tidings, and whom Lew had discipled. They have remained strong in their faith and in leadership with God's people. When I hear from or see them, we just take up where we left off the last time we talked. They are a joy in my life.

Our last "daughter" was Kathi, our redhead, who had the temperament to go with it. She and Mari Lou became "sisters" and Lew and I proceeded to tame our girl. We love Kathi. Because of her background she was very defensive, but the Lord helped us, and she stayed with it. Today Kathi is married to a wonderful man, and they live in New Brunswick. They have done terms in the North with the Royal Canadian Mounted Police, and she rescues deserted and abused dogs. They have three dogs of their own, including Lew's

Ssebo Sir. I had to give him up when I moved into this apartment. Kathi emails me, texts me, Skypes me, and sends me pictures. Without a doubt she became our second daughter—not the same as or own daughter Mari Lou, but lovable just the same.

The generations alive today need healing. Israel had disobeyed God, and a plague of snakes began to destroy them. God told Moses to make a brass serpent on a pole and tell the people to look at the serpent on the pole, and they would live.

> "As Moses lifted up the serpent in the wlderness,
> even so the Son of Man must be lifted up."
> —John 3:14

Jesus must be lifted up in the same way, not on a brass pole, but by us, declaring the power of His amazing grace. We who are alive in this generation have a responsibility to lift Jesus up for all to see Him and be healed from the attacks and lies of the wicked one—to look at Jesus now and live.

The Church is alive and well, the message of the Gospel has not changed, and the Holy Spirit has not changed. God is still using His servants to spread the Good News of His message to your town, and you are one of those servants.

Listen to what the spirit is saying to the church today. Go get them! Bring them into fellowship with Jesus. The church is not the building. The Church is *you* and every *believer*. The purpose is to bring all to Jesus, His truth living in their lives. The marriage supper of the Lamb will not be a wedding feast for a building. Jesus gave himself for the Church—His people, the Bride!

Around the world this generation has its own culture. It is not the same as it was in our generation. We must understand that God has always met every generation where they are so they can understand and receive. We must preach the Bible, the Full Gospel, but in a culture they understand. We must not compromise the message of our foundation, but leave aside our generational methods (that over the years we have become comfortable with) and adjust to the present day understanding.

Our faith is our foundation, the badge of true believers. Preserve it, preach it, teach it, live it, serve it to your community, demonstrate it by your works, and spend more time out among the people than you do in your office or church building. Our goal is not to fill our church buildings, but to turn our world to Jesus. Then the church building will fill up so fast we won't know where to put all the believers.

Jesus receives the glory, and He receives the honor. He gave His life on the Cross for me! Oh, the power in *His Redemptive Grace!* He alone is worthy!

Run Bible Church in YMCA Basement

Land for Permanent Building

Run Bible Church

Run Bible Church Opening
Permanent Building, 2005

Run Bible Church

First Institute Class

Graduation

Institute & Gardens

My JOY is Complete

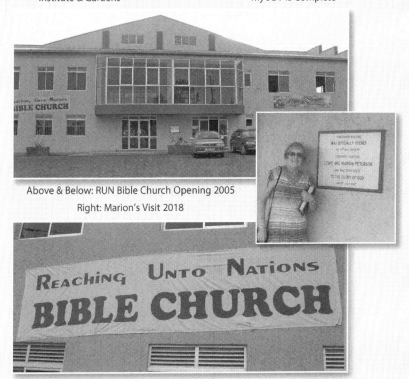

Above & Below: RUN Bible Church Opening 2005
Right: Marion's Visit 2018

All Hail King Jesus

All hail King Jesus, All hail Immanuel,

King of Kings, Lord of Lords,

Bright Morning Star.

And through all eternity, I'm going to praise Him,

And forevermore I will reign with Him.

There is coming a day when time shall be no more,

When the clouds shall be rolled back as a scroll.

Then the Lord shall appear in all His glory,

With ten million saints, singing love's sweet story.

—David Moody
(Used by permission)

Afterword

After Lew had passed, Mari Lou asked, "Mother, promise me something, I know you would like to live in a small apartment, but will you wait for a year before you make any major changes—give yourself time to grieve, please?"

I answered, "I promise."

The longest and hardest year of my life passed, and now I am in a lovely senior apartment in Chilliwack, B.C., Canada. The mountains surround me in a place with a small town feel, and it's just an hour or so from the beautiful Pacific Ocean, and Vancouver, where I grew up. I love the Fraser Valley! I keep believing that, "As the mountains are round about Chilliwack, so the Lord is round about His people."

I am so grateful for the overwhelming, unconditional, amazing grace of God. His grace and love called me to Himself and gave me the honor and privilege to be called to preach and teach in His Church in so many Nations. As the memories flood back and actually overtake my thoughts, I am humbled.

I have never been this old before, so I have no idea how I should feel—but I am in pretty good shape and feel great. Oh, the usual old age stuff is present, but nothing that the Lord and I can't handle.

Now what?

I don't know! But I do " . . . know whom I have believed, and am persuaded that He is able to keep what I have committed to Him until that day."

My desire is not to repeat history, but to move on into what God has for today. To the next generation I say, "It's your turn now!" I am delighted to share what I have learned in my sixty years of full-time ministry. It wasn't a perfect life by any means. Mistakes were probably too abundant, but we also learned from them. We were a team with a vision, and we followed our dreams one step at a time while the Spirit spurred us on. Feel free to call or text me.

Abundant blessings,

Marion Layzell-Peterson

marionp1938@gmail.com

APPENDIX 1

Jesus Is Alive!

Jesus freely, with joy, sacrificed his life for the world—the supreme sacrifice. He died and was buried... but... HE ROSE AGAIN, demonstrating His power to share His eternal life with the human race once and for all!

It is finished! No more need for other blood to be sacrificed, or for a life to be taken to cover man's sins. He offers the power of redemptive grace! It is free. Eternal life for all who believe.

"For God so loved the world that He gave
His only begotten son
that whosoever believes in Him shall not perish
but have everlasting life."
—John 3:16

His birth was announced by heaven.

"For there is born to you this day in the city of David
a Savior, who is Christ the Lord"
Suddenly there was with the angel a multitude
of the heavenly host praising God saying:

"Glory to God in the Highest, and on earth peace,
goodwill toward men!"
—Luke 2:11–14

His resurrection was confirmed by heaven.

Early on the first day of the week…women came to the
tomb …they found the stone rolled away…they entered the
tomb and did not find the body of Jesus…they were greatly
perplexed…saw two men in shining garments standing by…
they were alarmed and he said: "You seek Jesus of Nazareth,
who was crucified. Why do you seek the living among the
dead? He is not here, He Is Risen!"
—Mark 16:6; Luke 24:5–6

"If Christ is not risen, your faith is futile;
you are still in your sins
But Christ is risen from the dead.
For as in Adam all die, so in Christ
all shall be made alive."
—1 Corinthians 15:17, 20, 22

The Disciples were with Jesus 40 days, and then, while they
watched, He was taken up to heaven, and those two men in shining
garments appeared again!

"…This same Jesus, who was taken
up from you into heaven,
will so come in like manner as you saw
Him go into heaven."
—Acts 1:11

What grace! What power! His redemptive grace. His saving,
redeeming power. Every possession incorporated in His Name
belongs to us through his sacrifice and His resurrection life—so
amazing. All we believers have to do is believe and act, by faith in
Him, upon that provision. It is already ours!

"But we see Jesus, who was made a little lower that the angels,
for the suffering of death crowned with glory and honor,
that He, by the grace of God, might taste death for everyone."
—Hebrews 2:9

"Having boldness to enter the holiest by the blood of Jesus,
by a new and living way which He consecrated for us."
—Hebrews 10:19, 20

"For I am not ashamed of the gospel if Christ,
for it is the power of God to salvation
for everyone who believes."
—Romans 1:16

Believe it. It is for real.

APPENDIX 2

Timeline

Lewis is born—Lethbridge, Alberta	February 27, 1937
Marion is born—Toronto, Ontario	June 19, 1938
Lewis begins First Grade—Vancouver, BC	1942
Marion Begins First Grade—Wiarton, Ontario	1943
Lewis is a Brick Mason at Nels Peterson & Sons	1950–1959
Lewis & Marion studying at Glad Tidings Bible College	1952–1964
Lewis's Mason Apprenticeship Graduation	1955 (Vancouver Vocational Institute)
Marion's High School Graduation	1956
Marion, Cosmetologist at Vancouver Vocational Institute	1956–1958
Marion Layzell marries Lewis Peterson	February 14, 1958
Pastors in Abbotsford, BC	1958
Mari Lou is born	October 6, 1959
Lewis is ordained	1961
Marion is ordained	1964
Pastors, Gospel Mission to Uganda (East Africa)	1964–1968 (with ministry in Kenya, Mozambique, South Africa Zimbabwe & Israel)
Assistant Pastors / Youth Pastors, Glad Tidings Temple	1968–1978 (with ministry in USA, Taiwan, Canadian Arctic & Mexico)

USA residents, Traveling	1978
Pastors, Yuba City, California	1978–1984 (with ministry in Taiwan, Japan, Mexico & Canada)
Mari Lou Peterson marries Jeffrey Holmes	August 25, 1984
Pastors, Uganda 2, East Africa / RUN Ministries	1984–1998 (RUN Ministries: USA, England, France, Norway, Scotland, Belgium, Holland, Ireland, Republic of Congo, Tanzania, Rwanda, Burundi, Sudan)
Lewis & Marion earn BA in Theology (Christian International University, Santa Rosa Beach, Florida)	1989
Edward Stephan Holmes is born	April 23, 1989
Brian Reginald Holmes is born	September 21, 1991
Lewis: Staff Pastor, City Bible Church, Portland, Oregon	1998–2003 (Ministry in Ghana, Nigeria, Liberia, Puerto Rico)
Marion: Administrative Assistant	1998–2003 (Tri-County BCD; CALED.net; Washington School Board)
Lew-Mar Ministries, Chehalis/Centralia, Washington	2003–2010 (Ministry in Ethiopia, Malawi, Botswana, Romania, Hungary, Germany, Singapore, India, Korea, Brazil, Guatemala, Costa Rica, Panama, Columbia)
Lewis diagnosed / Retirement in BC, Canada	2010
Moved to Abbotsford, BC, Canada	2015
Moved to Chilliwack, BC, Canada	2016
Lewis to Heaven	March 8, 2017
Marion moves to Elim Village Apartment	May 17, 2018

Made in the USA
San Bernardino, CA
06 May 2020